MONASTIC WISDOM SERIES:

C000096421

Louis A. Ruprecht Jr.

An Elemental Life

Mystery and Mercy in the Work of
Father Matthew Kelty, OCSO
(1915–2011)

MONASTIC WISDOM SERIES: NUMBER FIFTY-SIX

An Elemental Life

Mystery and Mercy in the Work of Father Matthew Kelty, OCSO (1915–2011)

Louis A. Ruprecht Jr.

α

Cistercian Publications
www.cistercianpublications.org

LITURGICAL PRESS
Collegeville, Minnesota
www.litpress.org

A Cistercian Publications title published by Liturgical Press

Cistercian Publications
Editorial Offices
161 Grosvenor Street
Athens, Ohio 45701
www.cistercianpublications.org

Excerpts from Matthew Kelty, *Sermons in a Monastery: Chapter Talks*, edited by William O. Paulsell, © 1983; Matthew Kelty, *The Call of Wild Geese*, edited by William O. Paulsell, © 1996; Matthew Kelty, *Singing for the Kingdom: The Last of the Homilies*, © 2008; and Matthew Kelty, *Gethsemani Homilies*, edited by William O. Paulsell, © 2010, are used with permission of Cistercian Publications.

My Song is of Mercy by Matthew Kelty Copyright © 1994. Used by permission of Rowman & Littlefield Publishing Group. All rights reserved.

Excerpt(s) from HAUNTS OF THE BLACK MASSEUR: THE SWIMMER AS HERO by Charles Sprawson, copyright © 1992 by Charles Sprawson. Used by permission of Pantheon Books, an imprint of the Knopf Doubleday Publishing Group, a division of Penguin Random House LLC. All rights reserved.

© 2018 by Order of Saint Benedict, Collegeville, Minnesota. All rights reserved. No part of this book may be used or reproduced in any manner whatsoever, except brief quotations in reviews, without written permission of Liturgical Press, Saint John's Abbey, PO Box 7500, Collegeville, MN 56321-7500. Printed in the United States of America.

1   2   3   4   5   6   7   8   9

Library of Congress Control Number: 2018944702

ISBN 978-0-87907-056-4   ISBN 978-0-87907-656-6 (e-book)

This book is dedicated to my friend,
and Matthew's fellow-traveler,
Michael Bever

Now we have our brief moment here,
We came yesterday, are here today, will be gone tomorrow.
Let that brief moment be spent in communion
with the whole of life
so that we will not have lived in vain.

Father Matthew Kelty, OCSO

As a child I used often to go sit in the woods on the little hill back of the house. . . . And I remember consciously thinking, and I must have done so many times, that the world was very beautiful, but that people were not. I felt the world would have been so fine a place without them. I sometimes feel now that I was onto a truth, though I was yet to learn that I was people.

Matthew Kelty, "Flute Solo," in *My Song is of Mercy*, 52

Contact with elemental forces has a way of reducing life to fundamental questions. The sea, the mountains, the desert, the wilderness, have all been from ancient times the testing place of the spirit.

Matthew Kelty, "The Psalms as Prayer,"
from *Sermons in a Monastery*, 10

Life is not one-sided. It is ambivalent. . . . There is a kind of elemental dialogue that seems to be deep in the nature of all reality. It is a dialogue which implies not merely a meeting, but a meeting in which the truth emerges not from one dominating the other but from each meeting the other in love and communing, avoiding mere submergence and disappearance into the other, or forcing the partner to disappear into one's own being. There is a sense in which we must hold our ground and insist on the genuineness of what we are, but it is an insistence that takes into account the other's right also to be what he is. It is in the meeting that the whole truth is born.

Matthew Kelty, "Our Last Christmas with Dom James,"
from *Sermons in a Monastery*, 84

Monks see things the rest of us don't; they see visions from the supernatural world. They refine their spirit through solitude and reflection and restraint. We blunt ours through social contact, lack of reflection, and indulgence. And so they perceive things we ourselves are unable to. When someone is alone in a quiet room he can easily hear the clock ticking. If others enter, however, with the usual chatter and commotion, he no longer hears it. But the ticking is still there to be heard.

Constantine Cavafy, "Clearing the Ground"

Table of Contents

Dedication

It has been raining steadily for almost 36 hours. This morning toward the end of my meditation the rain was pouring down on the roof of the hermitage with great force and the woods resounded with tons of water falling out of the sky. It was great! A good beginning for a New Year. Yesterday in a lull I was looking across the valley at black wet hills, sharply outlined against the woods, and white patches of water everywhere in the bottoms: a landscape well etched by serious weather.

Thomas Merton, *Learning to Love*, 3

❖ ❖ ❖ ❖ ❖

I traveled to the Abbey of Gethsemani on Valentine's Day in 2013. It was a strangely disorienting trip, in the beginning. The daffodils that normally begin blooming in Atlanta at precisely that time had come three weeks early—as had the cherry blossoms in Washington, DC, well in advance of the festival organized each March to celebrate their evanescent beauty.

By contrast, when I landed in Louisville, KY, it had already begun to snow. By the time I arranged my rental car and got underway, it was snowing hard and sticking to the road. The back roads, sided by barren tracks of fallow and frozen farmland, made for hard, slow going. I arrived in tar-pitch darkness; the darkened church and tower loomed mute in a clouded, moonless sky. Supper had been served and cleared, and the long monastic silence that begins at 8:00 p.m. each evening was begun. An obviously weary staff took me to my room, made sure I was settled, then retreated into the shadows and the silence and sleep. It was an ominous experience, the power of such silence. This, as I began to understand, is central to the power of such monastic place.

I repeated my paces, returning to the closest small town not far from the abbey and looked for a place to eat. Forgetting that it was Valentine's Eve, I walked into a fairly ramshackle saloon with a very old wooden bar and streaky mirror running the length of the lounge. It was a hardscrabble bar, with a low-key restaurant attached, testifying to the hard lives farmers lead in these relative backwaters. Valentine's Eve or no, I was overdressed—having gone straight to the airport from work—and stood out sorely among the couples and groups of friends all waiting for their tables to clear. Reservations ran late that night, and I would need to wait to eat. I dutifully sat at the bar, immediately noticed an impressive collection of local bourbons against the glass, sampled several.

And, much to my surprise, I talked. The locals could not have been more friendly and engaging, curious as to who I was, what I was doing there, where I'd come from. The mention of Atlanta turned the conversation immediately to politics, and it was made abundantly clear to me that I was in a very red part of a very red state. We disagreed about many things (not all), but with a cordiality and spirited friendliness that disarmed and delighted. When asked where I was staying, I mentioned the monastery; they all knew of it, but none had visited—just five miles up the road. Called into the dining room, the group with whom I'd been chatting invited me to come back the next night for more conversation, and clearly meant it, paying my bar bill before they left.

I was seated late, finished last, and only vaguely recall the dazzling ice-journey back to Gethsemani. It was a strange and surreal taste of the place I'd first known primarily as the location of Thomas Merton's hermitage and retreat, home to his wide-ranging spiritual exercises. It took some time before I would learn that Merton's experience of the area had been not so very different from my own. And so the close attention to place, to surroundings both natural and cultural, will be one recurrent theme in what follows here.

The next morning dawned bright and crystalline, with early morning sunlight seeming to shimmer on the frozen hillside. I grabbed a coffee, then crunched around the grounds of the monastery for a while, waiting for the day to warm. My first glimpse of Merton's grave, so eloquent in its simplicity and proximity to the retreat house and refectory, was gratifying, though the morning turned rapidly warmer and the snow-scape turned to slush as I lingered. I opted to take a drive around this storied natural landscape since by then the roads were already clear and very nearly dry.

It was while I was on the road that my dear friend, Michael Bever, called to inform me that his driveway had just been cleared and that he would arrive at Gethsemani in several hours. He had first suggested this visit, and he had made all the arrangements, so to be there without him made hermitage seem orphanage for the time being. The first glimpse of Mike descending from his car confirmed that the trip, so difficult initially, would be auspicious. And it was.

We spent significant time walking the grounds together, and thanks to Brother Paul Quenon, we were taken on a tour of Merton's hermitage. As is his wont ("playing Merton roulette," he calls it, only half in jest), Brother Paul retrieved one of Merton's published journals that are kept there, turning to the date from that year. He read gracefully, and I was enthralled by a long serendipitous description of a hawk descending to kill a bird, then devouring it just outside of Merton's window where I was then seated at his desk, listening. The ensuing meditation on the circle of life that followed has stayed with me to this day. Merton's writing, at times almost scandalous in its intimacy and self-revelation, does that to you: it invites you into friendship, with the promise of greater intimacy to come. Whether it does come, you realize only gradually, is up to you, and depends on what you give.

Mike and I spent as much time away from the abbey as on the grounds. We sampled excellent bourbons in several nearby towns. We heard some wonderful music, enjoyed some superb food, had some hilarious further exchanges with our nearer barside neighbors. This all replicated my first day, but deepened and improved upon it. With Mike, the place was a very different kind of place; it still is. Over several days, we mapped out the vague outline of a book devoted to Father Matthew Kelty; we both agreed that it could not be a book about Thomas Merton, large as his presence looms, still, at Gethsemani and elsewhere.

Matthew and Merton were decidedly different people, but this much they shared: they both created an atmospherics of intimacy that seem to belie the normal expectations of monastic life. What Merton did in print, Matthew did in person. Matthew's homilies, at times almost scandalous in their intimacy and self-revelation, invite you into friendship, and the promise of greater intimacy to come. Whether it does come, you realize only gradually, is up to you; this, too, depends on what you give.

Mike gave a great deal to his friendship and love for Father Matthew. He would often drive three hours each way from his home in Mount Carmel, just to see and hear Matthew at the Mass. Matthew sang the Mass in the old Latin style, which he loved, and he would serve anybody; his was an open table. That is all of a piece with his convictions about universal salvation, and his openness to all varieties of religious expression. (Father Matthew once preached to a room full of bishops, Mike tells me, suggesting to his assembled guests that "hell, even Vodou is better than nothing!" I can imagine the twinkle in his eye as he said so.)

For Matthew Kelty, continuing—which is a far cry from finishing—the work of Thomas Merton was informed in large measure by "all that eastern stuff" (the Taoism, the Zen Buddhism, the Sufism, the poetry of all kinds) . . . his own demurrals notwithstanding. Matthew claimed not to know Zen at all ("that was Merton's thing"), but Mike assures me that he did. Even a casual conversation with Matthew made that clear—his elusive wisdom-style, his remarkable spiritual discernment, and his eye for the essential natural detail. Matthew also read a great deal of poetry, as a way of setting the tone when he preached, and the interplay of his impish informality with his rhetorical intensity and spiritual luminescence could be equally affecting. He was a mesmerizing speaker. He brought gifts to his table—the poetry, the preaching, his own quiet embodiment of the Gospel—and if you didn't want it, or didn't understand it, or didn't feel ready for it, that did not appear to bother him much. I am not a Catholic myself, though more than a decade at the Vatican Library and its Secret Archives, and several trips to the Abbey of Gethsemani, have left me with strong and lasting impressions. I think of what I am doing here as an ethnography of monastic life as much as it is an appreciation of Father Matthew's spiritual legacy.

Up to now, I have been describing my second visit to the Abbey of Gethsemani; by then Father Matthew had gone to eternity, as they say here. The first time I visited the abbey, Mike arranged for me to meet with Father Matthew. The visit was not long, scarcely an hour, but it went deep—which does not surprise. Matthew began with several stories about Thomas Merton, in case that was what I wanted to hear. When it became clear that I was as interested in his present as I was in Merton's past, then Father Matthew spoke quietly and candidly of his own life as a monk and a person of aspiring faith and spiritual discernment.

I was deeply moved by the encounter, and I did what academics in such situations tend to do: I sent him a copy of my first book. Father Matthew sent me a lovely note not long thereafter, suggesting (as I would hear and read many times subsequently) that he was no scholar, and that such things as Hegel and Nietzsche were well beyond his limited capacities. But then he commented, almost casually, about one of the appendices in which the central point of the book was summarized in a more concrete way—and so it was clear that he had understood everything I had done, or at least had tried to do. That he was a scholar, and a man gifted with a remarkably supple intellect, is one of the central convictions that has led me to write this book. That he is a spiritual writer worthy of discussion together with his more famous contemporary, Thomas Merton, is another.

Mike gave far more to his encounters with Father Matthew than I. As I have already said, he came to Gethsemani countless times, simply to hear Matthew preach and to see him officiate . . . and then later, to interview him on camera for a marvelous experimental film he entitled *This Lone Brightness*, a film that Mike has now made available for anyone on his website, "Sunyata Sandwich." That film is Mike's poetic testament to Father Matthew, born of his gradual realization as to the depth of Matthew's life and legacy. In the course of their deepening bond, Mike elected to join the Roman Church.

This book is, or at least it aspires to be, a prose poetic counterpoint to Mike's cinematic testimonial. It will not match the beauty, nor the freshness and vitality, of what Mike produced. But this book is similarly dedicated to Mike's vision and impressions. That Mike is a scholar, and a man gifted with a remarkably supple intellect, is another one of the central facts that gave birth to this book. I have lost track of how many books, authors, and films Mike has brought to my attention over the years—Merton, Matthew, Nishida, Nishitani, Hafez, Rumi, and so many more—but I have not lost track of how much they each have contributed to me. That Mike is a spiritual poet equal in stature to his dear friend and fellow traveler is what inspires this dedication.

This book, then, is for Mike.

LAR
The Abbey of Our Lady of Gethsemani
September 2017

Preface

The elemental solitude of the person is forever. We are,
as God is. We are immortal, as God is. We are unique,
as God is. Granted our being, our immortality, our
uniqueness are limited, they are genuine dimensions of
the human.

Matthew Kelty, "A Bonding Beauteous,"
from *Singing for the Kingdom*, 16

❖ ❖ ❖ ❖ ❖

During his three-year tenure at a small experimental monastic community in Oxford, North Carolina, Father Matthew Kelty was invited to speak at a local college. After his performance, a resident professor of English "described him as a poet, a dancer, and a singer."[1] That the three main elements of artistic creativity and production—words, movement, and music—should be so combined in one religious performer is remarkable. And so it was perhaps most clearly in *hearing* Father Matthew Kelty's *performance* of his written words that their full impact became clearest. Still, he is a spiritual *writer* of deep and abiding insight.

That is perhaps a surprising way to describe a man who is far less known than his close contemporary and fellow monk,

---

[1] This story is rehearsed by William O. Paulsell in Matthew Kelty, *Singing for the Kingdom: The Last of the Homilies*, MW 15 (Kalamazoo, MI: Cistercian Publications, 2008), ix.

Thomas Merton. Father Matthew produced only one book, after all, his probing 1973 spiritual autobiography, *Flute Solo*. That book was re-issued in 1994 [in a volume entitled *My Song is of Mercy*], with some sixty-nine later talks and sermons appended to it. Four more collections of homilies were to follow: *Sermons in a Monastery* (1983), *Gethsemani Homilies* (1991, enlarged in 2010), *The Call of Wild Geese* (1996), and *Singing for the Kingdom* (2008), to which I have just alluded. He also published one collection of letters: *Letters from a Hermit*, in 1983. The works are all relatively short: *Flute Solo* is just seventy-two pages in its current edition, and none of the others makes it to two hundred pages. They are works of startling insight, produced in the first blush of bright discovery. And this may account for their remarkable freshness.

The man we meet in these pages was described by his dear friend and chronicler, Mike Bever, as "a sort of mystic leprechaun." Getting to the essence of such a man in print Mike has likened to "capturing a lightning bug." The question of how to proceed here was the first, and foremost.

It is a central tenet of Roman Catholic ethics and piety that there are four natural, or "cardinal," virtues, already well enunciated by the Greeks and summarized brilliantly in Aristotle's *Nicomachean Ethics*: courage, moderation, justice, and practical wisdom. Father Matthew noted that *cardo* is the Latin word for *hinge*, and so he called them "pivotal virtues."[2] To that list the Christian tradition has appended three *supernatural* virtues, first described in epistolary prose by Saint Paul in his first letter to the Greek community in Corinth: these are faith, hope, and love.

This blending of pagan and Christian virtues, which is such a central achievement of Saint Thomas Aquinas, seems well suited to Matthew Kelty's persona and to his view of the spiritual life. He made much of the pagan Celts in his own personal and ancestral history, as we will see. I will turn to that matter first, in the Introduction.

---

[2] Matthew Kelty, "Foresight," in *Singing for the Kingdom*, 71.

With this constellation in mind, I have organized this book in two related parts: an "elemental" section comes first and contains four (natural) chapters; a "spiritual" section comes next with three (supernatural) sections. The introduction serves as my overview of Father Matthew, the man and the writer, and an initial impression of his profound importance; it will also provide me with an opportunity to introduce Matthew Kelty's extraordinary meditations on time. Human beings, in his determined view, are in time but not of time. They are of God, and like God, they are eternal beings. Death is the passage from human time to divine time—a passage to eternity, as he had occasion to say many times. "You rob this life of its inner meaning when you rob it of its eternal significance. . . . Our immortality is not negotiable."[3] This, I have come to see only gradually, is a deeply Catholic way of viewing the matter, this passage into eternity.[4]

But between the natural man and the spiritual man stood Thomas Merton, assigned to Father Mathew as his novice instructor when Father Matthew first joined the community of Gethsemani in 1960. Some years later, the circle would close, and Father Matthew would serve in the capacity of Merton's final confessor, before his departure for—and tragic death in—Bangkok in 1968. I have come to believe that, by tracing Father Matthew's shifting attitudes toward (and deepening appreciation of) Thomas Merton, we also steal a glimpse into

[3] Matthew Kelty, "Rehearsal for Reality," in *Singing for the Kingdom*, 127.

[4] This can be a powerful insight for one, such as myself, who is not Catholic. When my mother was nearing the end of her long battle with ovarian cancer, suffering multiple organ failure and placed on a respirator she had not wished to be on, my brothers and I consulted with a resident ethicist at the hospital, Saint Vincent's in New York City. I was concerned to honor my mother's wishes, but I was haunted by questions of time: whether this was the day she was supposed to pass on, or some other day. "In the face of eternity," the ethicist observed, "questions like today or next month cease to have real significance." It seemed, and still seems, a very Catholic way of moral reasoning, and I was deeply comforted by it. I remain grateful for the tradition that produced such a perspective.

Father Matthew's own complex spiritual development, his own nearly continual deepening. Father Matthew was a sharper, more impatient, and more riseable young man when he met Thomas Merton. The man we meet in these later sermons and spiritual soundings was the man who emerged through Merton's influence upon him and only, tragically enough, after his death.

No Merton, no Matthew—that is the idea. Merton was, in this sense, *pivotal*. I am not suggesting that Merton made Matthew a more spiritual man, whatever that would mean; not at all. Rather, Merton helped Matthew to see and to embrace the elemental man he already was. And in this way, Matthew was liberated, freed, and enabled to do something very different with his very different spiritual gifts.

This is not a book about Thomas Merton, though his presence is palpable throughout. That the two men may be discussed in tandem, however, is both tribute and testimony.

Introduction
An Elemental Life

The body repeats the landscape. They are the source of
each other and create each other. We were marked by
the seasonal body of earth, by the terrible migration of
people, by the swift turn of a century, verging on change
never before experienced on this greening planet.

Meridel Le Sueur,
"The American People and the Newly Come," 17

And, for that matter, what shaggy loins, in what
Hibernian bog, druidical forest, sunless fjord, Saxon
settlement by the Elbe's mouth or the dismal Jutish
coast, were ultimately answerable for me?

Patrick Leigh Fermor, *The Broken Road*, 34

❖ ❖ ❖ ❖ ❖

Father Matthew Kelty, of the Order of Cistercians of the
Strict Observance (OCSO), was elemental. It will take some
time to reflect upon, and hence to explain, what that curious
statement can mean.

Such a reference to "the elements" can be variously heard,
variously interpreted, variously understood. The word itself
is nearly poetic in its variety and range of meanings. To the
high school student of chemistry, it may call up harrowing
images of the periodic table with its hundred-plus elements,

1

the first thirty or so of which constitute the fundamental building blocks of the living, pulsing universe that we know and inhabit. Viewed through this lens, stars are the elemental engines that drive life and almost all cosmic creative process; their unimaginable internal infernos continually turn hydrogen and helium into heavier elements . . . until their density destroys them in those paradoxical destruction-events that make heavier elements[1] (and still later, organic matter)—and therefore life such as we know it—possible. Stars are elemental. Space is elemental. Black holes, quantum particles, dark matter—all of this is elemental.

The modern sciences of astronomy, biology, chemistry, physics, all teach that there is no creation without destruction. No life without death. There is no necessary contestation with theology here; it is more a matter of tweaking the language, adjusting the metaphors, admitting some poetic text to the visual image. Supplemented in this way, we might say that there is no salvation without tragedy. No Christ without a cross. And, as Father Matthew was fond of adding—or rather, of reminding—there is no mercy without a deep mystery. To ponder these paradoxes, much like pondering the vastness of space or the omnivorous consuming activity of stars and their strange offspring, is to engage the elemental, to engage in elemental reflection.

To ponder the mystery that things exist in the face of the possibility of nothingness is already to engage in philosophy.

---

[1] On September 14, 2015, scientists from Caltech and MIT affiliated with the Laser Interferometer Gravitational-Wave Observatory (LIGO) recorded the first measurement of gravitational waves, a phenomenon that Albert Einstein had predicted one hundred years before; they announced their findings on February 11, 2016, suggesting that the pulse had been caused by the collision of two black holes. Three of the LIGO scientists (Rainer Weiss, Barry Barish, and Kip Thorne) were awarded the 2017 Nobel Prize in Physics for these discoveries.

As of this writing, LIGO has recorded six such measurements in total, the last of which (on August 17, 2017) was caused by the collision of two neutron stars, an event that produced enormous quantities of heavier metals in the aftermath.

The early Greek philosophers proclaimed that philosophy was born of the experience of wonderment in the face of the reality of there being things at all; wonder was the very *archê* of all deep thinking.[2] The contemporary philosopher John Sallis has called our attention to the role that the imagination can and must play if we wish to do philosophy in a way that is attentive to, and open to, the wonder of cosmology and creation (both artistic creation and otherwise, which will be an important connection to be made here).[3] Anne Carson puts this in a pithier way, as she is a poet too. For Carson, the philosopher is simply "one who delights in understanding."[4]

Father Matthew insisted that he was no intellectual, and certainly no philosopher (see Appendix). It is one of the few statements he made repeatedly with which I will not only disagree, but go to some lengths to disprove:

> If we see ourselves called to a life of pondering, it is to see ourselves involved with elemental dialogue between God and humanity, earth and heaven, time and eternity, man and woman, matter and spirit, body and soul. . . . Jesus Christ is the Son of God and Son of Mary. Easily said. Well said. But it will mean nothing at all, be only a formula, if we do not ponder it. And that is what we are here for, to ponder a lifetime on mystery.[5]

---

[2] See for instance, Plato, *Thaeatetus* 155d, and Aristotle, *Metaphysics* 982b.

[3] John Sallis, *Logic of Imagination: The Expanse of the Elemental* (Bloomington, IN: Indiana University Press, 2012).

[4] Anne Carson, *Eros the Bittersweet: An Essay* (Princeton: Princeton University Press, 1986), x.

[5] Matthew Kelty, "The Feast of Mary," in *The Call of Wild Geese: Monastic Homilies*, ed. William O. Paulsell (Trappist, KY: Cistercian Publications, 1983), 30, 32. Later in this same collection, he will add the following:

> Think well on it. Both men and women are called upon to be like Jesus. This is a call to true wholeness.
>
> Our society cruelly divides heaven and earth, man and woman, male and female. Christ unites them. . . .
>
> When we reduce Christ to male as we tend to reduce all men to males, not to say women to females, we run contrary to the Gospel.

In fact, Father Matthew was a prodigious ponderer. He was endlessly fascinated by the fact that the world, and the heavens, and humanity exist. He was consumed with wonderment before nature: nature's raw power and beauty, especially the beauty that, he insisted, revealed enough of God's reality to make infinite mercy available to all those who are neither Christians nor philosophers. He was intrigued by what we are made of, by what inspires us, by what sets us off course. He was convinced that God lay at the very center of all reality, and that God's gravitational pull was nothing if not universal, unmitigated, outlandish, an all-encompassing love for every thing and every sentient being. Father Matthew's thinking thus turned repeatedly to eternal, and what I am calling "elemental," questions.

Father Matthew was an elemental thinker in another, less cosmic, and decidedly more earthbound way. He was emphatically historical in his orientation; he lived and breathed an *historical* faith. He wanted, and needed, to comprehend that of which we are made. He understood that every human being is a link in the chain of temporal being that joins the past to the future in a transcendent now. As one of my early mentors, Dr. Stuart Clark Henry (1914–1997), put the point to me repeatedly, "every point in time is equidistant from eternity, each moment potentially transparent to the everlasting mercy." Stuart was thinking about Dante, I believe, and channeling Augustine (who observed this of God: "whose center is everywhere and whose circumference is nowhere").

Stuart and Matthew were contemporaries, born just one year apart, although separated by the vast cultural divide of the Mason-Dixon. Matthew was Boston-bred, and Stuart was emphatically of the Carolinas (where Matthew also spent three

---

In a word, Christ was both masculine and feminine because he was a complete human being, perfect.

This integrative (and elemental) image is from "Christ and the Family," in *The Call of Wild Geese*, 23–24.

years in an experimental and short-lived Cistercian community). But Stuart also loved Rome immoderately, and the
liturgy, and the Vatican, traveling there each year with his
sister. Father Matthew would have been finely attuned to
Stuart's mature ideas about time, transparency, mercy, eternity.
In a splendid meditation on the Feast of the Immaculate Conception in 1988, Father Matthew began, as he so often did, with
death and remembrance:

> One Veteran's Day, the former Armistice Day, November
> 11th, a monument to Vietnam veterans was dedicated in
> Frankfort, a work sponsored by the efforts of Ron Ray, friend
> of the Abbey. It is a large sundial on the Capitol grounds,
> with the names of 1046 war dead inscribed in rows on stone
> slabs in such a way that the sun's shadow from the gnomon
> point of the dial crosses the name of each on the day he died.
> So young Kentucky fallen are remembered.
>
> What does it mean? A shadow crossing a name, shadow
> from a sun 93 million miles away, its light eight minutes in
> reaching us. Are these notings of name and time real? Once
> we are gone, our dust too disintegrated, what does it mean
> to be remembered in human years or incised in stone, re-
> called on the altar?
>
> It does not mean much of anything unless time be some-
> thing nearly a delusion, a construct we use to deal with life
> as we know it, not unlike marking distance by inches and
> feet and yards, rods and miles, changing space not a whit,
> yet somehow necessary for us.[6]

Father Matthew is, as always, elemental in his way of looking at things. He does not just see the shadow and the stone;
he gazes more deeply in order to see sunlight and cosmic dis-
tance, the mystery of the universe's immensity and our virtual
invisibility within it. This gazing into depth creates new insight. And somehow, he brings it all back around to the Virgin

---

[6] Matthew Kelty, "Immaculate Conception," in *My Song is of Mercy*, ed.
Michael Downey (New York: Sheed and Ward, 1994), 159.

Mary, upon whom he meditated a great deal and with transparent adoration:

> We celebrate the conception of the Virgin Mary, the Mother of God. This is a yearly commemoration of an event we know in our faith to have taken place. Our faith is nothing if not historical, and this feast is to attest to it. It is our memorial Mass, an anniversary, our inscription in stone, a shadow from light passing over a person. Theologians of an earlier time were much puzzled for explaining how what happened did happen. For they figured time linearly in a rather narrow sense, and so were at a loss to know how the Redemption could take effect before it happened. Later theologians said it was "anticipated," and that proved satisfactory. Today, we might not be so skittish, for our views of time change and we are not so sure anymore that time is always before and after. For God surely, for us also. Conception is not temporal, but is an entry into eternity. Time is but an Advent before birth.[7]

So much for not being a philosopher. In very short order, Father Matthew has walked us through several deep theological conundrums and their partial resolution; he has gestured lightly to the Einsteinian revolution in thinking about time and space and concluded with a loving gesture to the Virgin Mary. "Every point in time is equidistant from eternity, each moment potentially transparent to the everlasting mercy."

Father Matthew knew this, understood it capaciously, and believed it to be historical fact. This, I think, is what gave him

---

[7] Kelty, "Immaculate Conception," 159; see also "Immaculate Conception, B.V.M.," 182–83. See also "Times," in *My Song is of Mercy*, 204:

There is linear time. There is cyclic time. And there are other times as well. But what concerns us today is God's time. Perhaps we could call it liturgical time, dream time, festal time. . . . [W]hen we celebrate Christ, we do so in a quite different way. We enter into a kind of dream time, our first modest taste of eternity, in which history disappears and what was past becomes present, remote becomes here. For we deal with realities so deep, so profound that one encounter would scarcely do. We need to return again and again if we are to enter into them.

his rich sense of tradition, of culture, of identity, of the depths that comprise us and in which we find our ground. He spoke often of "the deeps," and so will I. "There is a you deep down within," he observes, "something real and immortal and touched with the divine. Touched, indeed. Possessed by the divine. Loved by the Lord God and wrapped in his presence."[8] That touch, too, is decidedly historical. Deep down, Father Matthew Kelty was Irish:

> So there is a point to pride in being Irish and an inheritor of the Celtic charism. There is honor in being Catholic and a member of Christ. We do sense glory in being Benedictine and in living a tradition 1,400 years old. So too we share a certain aura in being Cistercian, members of an Order over 900 years old, who live in a house where the praise of God has been chanted seven times a day for over 150 years.[9]

Father Matthew understood himself to be embedded in a mystifyingly long and complex history of predecessors; he inhabited that sensibility with an uncanny sense of piety. Piety, after all, is the virtue of living in the face of debts (or depths) and gratitudes we cannot reasonably hope to repay. "To be sure," Matthew continues with a wink, "our glory in all the above is as much gratitude to God as anything else for reason of having had so little to do with it."[10]

We are meant to consider this closely. In short order, Father Matthew has identified himself as participant in a Christian tradition some 2000 years old, a Benedictine tradition some 1400 years old, a Cistercian tradition some 900 years old, and a monastic community in Kentucky more than 150 years old. Now *that* is being a link in a chain.

---

[8] Matthew Kelty, "The Monastic Technique," in *Sermons in a Monastery: Chapter Talks*, ed. William O. Paulsell, Cistercian Studies 58 (Kalamazoo, MI: Cistercian Publications, 1983), 29.

[9] Matthew Kelty, "Bernard II," in *Gethsemani Homilies*, ed. Willam O. Paulsell (1991; rev. ed. Kalamazoo, MI: Cistercian Publications, 2010), 105.

[10] Kelty, "Bernard II," 106.

But this list of pious regard begins by sounding a more un-usual note. What in the world, we may wonder, is "the Celtic charism," that is, the singular grace of "being Celtic." For so he was. The Kelty clan, as he never tired of coyly reminding his friends and auditors, was a Keltic clan. What role does this element, a decidedly pre-Christian element, play in his life and way of thinking? A great deal, in the end.

As he would reflect many times, this "Celtic charism" was pagan, and pre-Christian. This is all rather striking meditation in a monk:

> People from Ireland some three thousand years before Christ built massive mounds of stone, hills with a hidden, inner chamber for the dead. The blind entry passage had a slot over the barred door that admitted sunlight, sunlight that at Newgrange on December 21, the winter solstice, would pass through the slot, go down the corridor and flood the inmost chamber with light, once a year.
>
> What an observant people! How carefully they watched the movement of sun and moon and stars. How shrewd in their ability to build a small hill and equip it with so elabo-rate a design. Much of the interior was carved with intricate patterns.
>
> What were they saying in all of this if not expressing hunger for light, not merely the phases of the sun's light, the moon's light, the light of the stars, but a different light that would never be overcome with darkness. Surely this is all prophetic, this is the human heart dreaming of a coming day, which would know no end, the perpetual light to which we commend the dead.
>
> It is to be noted, of course, that all this is for northern lati-tudes, whose winter knows no green, enters into long nights and short days this season. It does not follow that lower latitudes and people on the other side of the world have no way of saying what we say. Christ is for all, for everyone, everywhere.[11]

---

[11] Matthew Kelty, "Trees," in *Gethsemani Homilies*, 65.

There is a lot going on in this brief passage, and it begins, suggestively, with a cosmic observation. God, as Father Matthew never tired of reminding his listeners (he is rehearsing the first chapter of Paul's Letter to the Romans here), revealed Godself sufficiently in creation for all the world to awe at. But Father Matthew sees more than this. He sees the ancient Celtic peoples striving and aspiring to the divine light, actually hungering for it. It is not that they were Christians before their time and without their knowing; it is rather that they were divinized before Christian time, touched by that same everlasting mercy. God's time is not linear. Matthew's universalism insists, with the canonical gospels, that Christ lost not one of those whom God entrusted to him.

And this is why Matthew Kelty was so captivated by the image of Holy Saturday (he spoke of it often[12]), when Christ is alleged to have descended into, and "harrowed," Hell. In other words, the pre-resurrection Christ went down, in order to bring everyone up, to make his mercy available to those who came before his coming. Christ fills the space between each link of that historical chain, forging it into an unbreakable instrument of mercy.

It cannot be accidental that Ireland is one of those unusual places in which the Christianization of the land came effortlessly, almost drowsily, *without martyrdom*. There is little doubt that, in the lands where Christians were persecuted as a counter-culture, there the dominant culture that vilified them was recalled later as a distinct problem. Greeks needed to break with their Hellenism; Romans needed to break with their *Romanitas*. Conversion for these people was described as a partial death to one's former self and culture. Not so in the fortunate lands that sidestepped martyrdom and empire. There, everything speaks of subtle cultural *continuity*, not dramatic rupture. Father Matthew would generalize this point

[12] See, for instance, "Mystical Time," and "Paschal Vigil," in *Gethsemani Homilies*, 48, 83, and "The Greatest of the Sacraments," in *Singing for the Kingdom*, 95.

and this experience, making it the very essence of the Gospel's spread, and of his own vernacular credo:

> . . . the sending of the Spirit, the birth of the Church, the writing of the Scriptures—all these marvelous mythic-historic doings entered into the very heart and life of the people. An entering into the heart, no mere appendage, some veneer on the surface. It was deep precisely because all these truths responded to primeval myths that rose from human depths and took various shapes and forms among various peoples. Christianity did not need to crush these myths: it answered them, fulfilled them, supplanted them with something richer and more complete. That is why Europeans accepted the faith with such ease. . . .[13]

Not all Europeans, we should want to add, but perhaps the Irish. In a word, Celtic Christians remained Celts, and embraced their Christianness in a Kelt-y way. It all sounds rather effortless, easy, spirit-infused. "What a monastery does is create a climate in which communion with the world of spirit is easy and normal," he observes. "Natural. A primitive village is like that. Celtic Ireland was like that."[14]

And yet. Ireland, in Father Matthew's telling, was also a tortured land of suffering, pain, tragedy[15] —as he notes in one of the most jarring statements he ever made about the Irish:

---

[13] Matthew Kelty, "Dreams and Visions and Voices," in *My Song is of Mercy*, 83.

[14] Matthew Kelty, "All Souls Day," in *The Call of Wild Geese*, 61.

[15] See "A Glorious Prelude," in *Singing for the Kingdom*, 57: "I mean to say, the Irish seem endowed with a sense of the tragic. Though everything's just fine for now it won't last. Something is bound to happen that will spoil it. It's waiting its turn in the wing. As an intimate of Kennedy at the scene in Dallas said, 'We knew it wouldn't last, but I just didn't think it would come so soon.'

It may all be Irish fantasy. Suffering and disappointment touches everyone, after all."

Surely [the Irish] are a people beloved of God, surely a people blessed with kinship to the world of the spirit, a people of the wind and the rain and the sea, of remote islands, dynamically communal and passionately solitary. They are great fighters, great poets, gifted in speech, in human encounter, in humor.

If they have been so blessed, then why so cursed? . . .

To this people dearly beloved by God and so heavily burdened, a sweet Providence sent, 150 years ago in 1845, a five-year famine that left at least one million dead and drove abroad two million more. So what have we done to deserve this? One does not speak so, even when famine was followed by the severest winter in history with mild westerlies replaced by snow-bearing gales from the plains of Russia that brought six inches of snow to Ireland.

Instead of complaint, look around. There are millions of Irish all over the world, and where the Irish went, the faith went. They brought their gifts and graces to many lands. This was the fruit of starvation and tyranny. In the eighteenth, nineteenth, and twentieth centuries, seven million Irish came to this country alone. Their descendants are some forty million today. . . .

The lesson is clear. Bear what must be borne for Christ's sake, in the hope that somehow, somewhere, sometime, great good will come of it.

This is not Irish superstition; it is the faith. It is to reconcile peace and joy with suffering and death. The road is rough and the gate narrow, and I don't think it can be other than that, can it?[16]

God's providential care for the Irish took the form of rapine and pillage, famine and flood. The Irish spirit bore this all with an intriguing blend of stoic (or is it Celtic?) resolve and Christian charity. When necessary, they left their homes and carried their Celtic Christianity with them. And it has flourished

---

[16] Matthew Kelty, "A Call Universal and Unique," in *Gethsemani Homilies*, 41–42.

everywhere it went . . . including, we are meant to understand, in Father Matthew's very own backyard, in Boston. In
fact, the Irish translocation to the New World is what made
Matthew Kelty possible; he would have come into existence
in no other way or form. This is elemental. And he dares to
call it grace.

This quite suddenly seems like a very hard gospel, as hard
to bear as life itself: "It is a hard day for many people. It is a
world full of mystery and darkness. The Lord made the night
too long for some people. And that is only the beginning."[17]
Father Matthew's writing has a way of sneaking up on you,
catching you by surprise. He often begins in surprising, oblique
ways that seem unrelated to the topic at hand. His juxtaposi-
tions can seem strange, or happenstance, or simply hard to
follow. But then quite suddenly, the key turns in the lock. A
Kentucky war memorial is relevant to the Virgin Mary. The
greatest trickster of all is death, but he is a mere prelude to
infinite mercy. It is in and through death that one passes from
time to eternity, an altogether different temporal mode. This
seems to be a distinctively Catholic way to think about it.

There is a dark ellipsis in the passage with which I have just
been struggling here, and it is striking for how differently it
scans from Matthew's more general, and very nearly instinc-
tive, humanism:

> If they have been so blessed, then why so cursed? Why are
> they so misery-ridden? The English are Teutonic and the
> Irish Celt. They do not meet. They live in different worlds.
> They do not understand one another. Good enough; people
> differ. But the Irish were miserably oppressed by the British
> for seven centuries. More than that, oppressed because they
> were Catholic. The Irish never had a colony because they
> never were a country, never oppressed another people be-
> cause they were never there to oppress.[18]

---

[17] Matthew Kelty, "The Poor Monk," in *Sermons in a Monastery*, 5.
[18] Kelty, "A Call Universal and Unique," in *Gethsemani Homilies*, 41–42.

Why do the Irish suffer? Because there are the English. This is a strikingly one-sided account; there is little of the elemental dialogue that Father Matthew normally calls for,[19] and precious little charity. English and Irish: to Father Matthew's way of thinking, the cultural strain was past bearing, and the religious divide complete; one oppressor, one oppressed. (Later, he would observe that Thomas Merton was English, unlike his Celtic confessor.) It is not easy to know what to say about this observation, and I suspect that Father Matthew pondered the paradox fairly often himself. Perhaps this brief excursus into Irish history owes more to Father Matthew's immersion in the Hebrew Bible, especially the Psalms. Lamentation was a core religious modality for him.[20]

If we square the English with the Romans, and the Irish with the Judeans, then perhaps we can make better sense of the idea. For we know that the Romans had a very different story about what went wrong in Judea.[21] They did not see their actions as oppression, nor did they intend it as such. Their interest was in religious accommodation; the Judeans did not wish to be so accommodated. No one started this fight; it was elemental.

So in using Jewish history as a way to make sense of the Celtic claim, Father Matthew seems to derive a lesson: the Irish church may have been a church without martyrdom . . . and

[19] Matthew Kelty, "Being in Relation," in *My Song is of Mercy*, 188: "So take this home with you. The solitude of the human is a duality. We are never, can never be alone. That is why monks love solitude. It proves that what we've been saying all along is true: there's always two. There's always the other."

[20] Matthew Kelty, "For Charlie+/Jeremiah 20," in *My Song is of Mercy*, 168–71.

[21] We possess several intriguing Roman observations on Judeans and Judaism, such as the fifth book of Tacitus, *The Histories*, trans. Kenneth Wellesley (New York: Penguin Books, 1964), 271–79, and several legal codes that betray an interest in circumcision and the apparent cultural exceptionalism it was deemed to represent. But the finest rendition I know is fiction: Marguerite Yourcenar, *Memoirs of Hadrian*, trans. Grace Frick with the author (New York: Farrar Straus Giroux, 1957), 233–51.

hence there was no need to break with the Before, but the Irish land and the Irish people were crucified all the same.

If that is the idea here, then we come to the crossroads of another problem: there can be a subtle oppression in every claim to universalism. Put your arm fondly upon my shoulder and say that we are all one. What must I give up in order to accept this claim? How much did the Canaanites or the Philistines give up to David's and Solomon's empire, armed with its "universalizing" mission before God? How much must the pre-harrowed in hell give up in order to take Christ's outstretched hand? This much we do know: Israel has always been the fly in the theological ointment of the Christian Church, the one indigestible element for Rome, when Rome was not yet Christian . . . as well as when she was.[22] It is striking, in general, how little monastic reflection on Jews and Judaism, apart from the Psalms, there has been.[23] Thomas Merton thought a great deal about eastern Buddhists, and Father Matthew thought a great deal about the western Celtic peoples (both of them primal, in their way), but they do not seem to have thought a great deal about Judaism's place in the complicated arc of grace, the salvation history in which they both believed. Salvation, Father Matthew insisted, was universal

[22] I am indebted to a relatively new book by John G. Gager, *Who Made Early Christianity? The Jewish Lives of the Apostle Paul* (New York: Columbia University Press, 2015), for a remarkable account of the way in which Paul understood Israel's covenantal relationship with God to be unchanged, but to have been supplemented now with a new way open to such relation for Gentiles . . . as well as how Paul's enduring Judaism was later misunderstood, ignored, and corrupted.

[23] I have in mind comments like the following, which begin with reflections on "primitive thinking" and border on supersessionism: "It is very necessary when reading or hearing the Old Testament stories, to keep in mind that it is the Old Testament. And the Old Testament has been completed and fulfilled, if not corrected, in the New. The Old must always be read in terms of the New. The psalms the monks love so must always go hand-in-hand with the Gospels; otherwise their often violent and vivid language may lead us to omit parts and will be misleading. . . . We do not live in the Old Testament, but in the New" (Matthew Kelty, "Evil's Return," in *My Song is of Mercy*, 177–78).

or it was not at all. There is indeed a place, or rather a dimension, which we call hell, just as surely as there is evil in every human heart; we simply cannot say if there is anyone there.[24]

Father Matthew resolved this tension within Christian universalism in a remarkable way, a way that brought it into subtler alignment with Judaism. He turns the grasping hand into an outreach and embrace. In point of fact, he *reconceived* Christian monotheism. When we read the Hebrew chronicles, what we see is an ancient version of the "culture wars." Monotheism appears to mean one-and-only-one-God-ism; if you do not venerate our God, then you have no God. The Other as atheist, worthy of annihilation.

Father Matthew sees this all quite differently. God, the singular and loving focal point of all creation, is not simply *one*; God is *unique*. *Mono-* means singular, not single, not one-and-only. God's creativity thus revels in *singularities*, a word very fond to modern astrophysicists: no two beings are composed of the elements in quite the same way. This next passage appears in the context of Matthew's meditation on "elemental dialogue," a dialogue that must take trouble to avoid reducing one to another, the other to the self, the different to the same:

> Uniformity, then, is not characteristic of the work of God. It is only a human being who cares to turn out a million cans of tomato soup and takes pride in the undoubted truth that one tastes exactly like another. God, on the contrary, delights in variety. He does not delight in uniformity and repetition. So simple a thing as an oak leaf must be unique and singular, different from every other oak leaf. God takes glorious delight in the individual, the specific.[25]

[24] Matthew Kelty, "The Lord of Glory," in *Gethsemani Homilies*, 81: "That there is a hell, we know. Whether any human is there or not or will be, we do not know. That one can choose hell, we also know." And also "Joseph," in *Gethsemani Homilies*, 89: "All our prayers are plural. We exclude none. We include all. We want none to go to hell. We would have all saved. It is healthy to keep such a vision bright, to keep our piety generous."

[25] Matthew Kelty, "Our Last Christmas with Dom James," in *Sermons in a Monastery*, 84.

Mono-theism then, inflected in Father Matthew's Celtic-monastic-idiomatic way, implies monopersonalism, the fact that a singularity is precious precisely because it is unique. "People," he continues, "are fearful of the different." God, by contrast, appears to revel in it. That is the core truth to which all of creation ultimately attests. There are finite elements; none of them are combined the same way twice. One God mysteriously erupts outward into the comparative infinity of a highly pluralist creation.

Matthew came upon his interest in the Greek prefix *mono-* quite early in his eremitic career. During Holy Week of 1973, shortly after being posted as a solitary in Papua New Guinea, he composed a moving series of meditations, entitled *Flute Solo*:

> Quite by accident, I stumbled onto a happy word in a Greek dictionary, *monaulia*, "flute solo." But it has another definition as well, "the solitary life," since the root means both "flute" and "house," and the *monos* characterizes the solo flute and the person living alone, the solitary. It is a beautiful combination, for both are a kind of poetry. Certainly neither has any great practical value, yet the world would be less charming for want of the flute, less tolerable if there were no hermits.[26]

The note nicely captures a juxtaposition with which he toyed throughout his life: religion and art, two unique and related forms of spiritual creativity. (The Romantics would add philosophy to this august list, and I suppose so would I. I have already said that Matthew was a philosopher, even if he does not mention philosophy here.) Matthew Kelty lived the monastic life artfully, with tremendous creativity and uncanny

[26] Matthew Kelty, "Flute Solo," in *My Song is of Mercy*, 2. He was later to observe, "one needs a sort of compassion for poets and priests and artists. We do not realize what a precious gift they are to humanity. Or what a burden they bear" (58).

intentionality. His wisdom was borne of these artful and religious resources. His writing, his reflection, his homilies, even his silence, were pregnant with poetic artistry. For this artistic soul, mono-theism meant that God is singular, solitary, and yet paradoxically reaching out in loving connection with all being. So should we all be.

There is more to say about Father Matthew's interest in his Celtic roots, to be sure. Curiously, he never really talked about Ireland's patron saint, Patrick. I suspect this is because Matthew *liked* snakes. He certainly understood Ireland's definitive position and posture as an island, a water-place, a place alternately blue and green. And he recalls it is a place of dark, heroic humor, something very much akin, as we shall see, to *monastic* humor:

> It's the way it was with Brother. He was young and went about his business like any other monk. Only they made him an electrician because the monk who had been the electrician before him got the idea that there was nothing to do but listen to God telling him to get out of the monastery. He did, and God be with him, but that left us without an electrician.
>
> I do not know how you do it, but our method is direct. When you run out of something, you call a relatively simple, unassuming and submissive monk and you tell him, "Brother, you are now the electrician." A few facts, such as he knew nothing about electricity, proved only that Brother was being irrelevant, and if there is anything one must be these days it is relevant. So Brother said OK, he was the electrician.
>
> He did all right and bravely went about the monastery changing light bulbs and bit by bit advancing into more mysterious areas. The only blunder I know of was when he pulled a plug out of the side of something in the cheese plant and released the ammonia in the refrigerating unit, which could have been bad but did no more than strip three big trees in back of the library and kill them outright. So Brother kept doing his job like anyone else.

One day an X-ray truck came and offered to take our pic-
tures, so we all had our lungs photographed. A few months
later the results came back. Brother had on his lungs funny
spots over which many doctors frowned many times. So
they took him to Louisville, and the grim word came back.
They opened him up and took one look and sewed him
together again. He was full of cancer. Figure that out and
you won't be scared anymore.[27]

This is not so much tragic as it is absurd. It is a story worthy
of Samuel Beckett. Jewish humor has nothing on the Irish. We
all must go to ground. "Death always means God," Father
Matthew tells us, strangely, "and the question always is, 'Is he
angry? Did he do it on purpose?' And the suspicion always is,
'Yes, he is. And he did.' And so we try very hard to get something between that worry and ourselves. Something we can
hang death on."[28] Father Matthew's purpose here is to make
the rather Protestant-seeming point that there is nothing that
can get between you, and your mortality, and the divine. Thus,
"if we are to deal with death, . . . we must go ever so much
deeper."

Father Matthew went to the Eucharist, as often as not, whose
elements provide the most elemental kind of therapy in the
face of death. His rhapsodic eulogy is as follows:

It is also sacrifice. There is altar. There is priest. There is
victim. And immolation. And only after that, communion.

And we are not watching something. We are doing something. We are going back to our primordial past[,] to the day
we put Christ to death. And by that fact learned to die. Death
entered the world by sin. Also ours. The old legend is neat.
When they dug the hole for the Cross, they found the skull
of Adam; our history is one piece. But the mystery we enter

[27] Kelty, "The Poor Monk," in *Sermons in a Monastery*, 4.
[28] Matthew Kelty, "No Poison, This Mercy," in *My Song is of Mercy*, 97.

into is also a mystery of mercy. He has forgiven us. And the
proof is the eating and the drinking of his Body and Blood.

So we do not have to ask about someone "What did they
die of?" They died of sin. Along with the Galileans and those
by the tower in Siloam. Along with Michael and Louis
[Thomas Merton] and absolutely everyone else. . . . Here
at the altar, we face the issues and live reality. If we put
Christ to death, that ought to end it: no need now to put
myself to death, or others. No need for violence against
myself or others. No need to punish, to bring to heel, to take
to task, to shape up or bring into line this mess that is life
because I hate it and everyone in it. No need for the war we
love, communal, familial, national. We've done all that, seen
all that—*deja vu*. It is, rather, time to breathe fresh air and
see wide views, and know a warm sun rising in the east.
Because mercy has become the climate in which we live.
Which is to say, we know what it means to repent: it means
to accept mercy. Otherwise, we perish.[29]

It is instructive to notice the poetic arc of this essay. And it
is an essay—a foray, an attempt to grapple with a mystery. It
begins with the brute fact of death. It moves to ritual, the
human artistry with which mystery is best apprehended
("Cavalry in real time," Matthew once quipped about the
Mass). And it concludes with elemental vision: breeze, landscape, sun, the new climate of mercy. Plato suggested that to
say what the human soul is would require a god's view of the
matter. But people are virtuosic in metaphor, in saying what
things are like.[30] Augustine agreed; if you understood a description of God, then it was not God you were describing.[31]

The ancients, and most notably Father Matthew's ancient
Celtic forebears, also spoke of "the elements," but they did not

[29] Kelty, "No Poison, This Mercy," 97–98; see also "Hatred of God," in *The Call of Wild Geese*, 87.

[30] Plato, *Phaedrus* 246a.

[31] Matthew Kelty, "Ash Wednesday," in *Gethsemani Homilies*, 35.

know our periodic table. Like the cardinal virtues, their elements were four in number: earth, water, air, fire. Combined in much the same manner as we imagine our atoms in combination, these elements made life possible, gave it order, and disorder, and mystic, tragic meaning. Father Matthew pondered long and deeply on these verities, the elements of which we are all composed. True to that Celtic spirit, I will offer some reflections with him, through these elements of his writing and reflection. They will be short. And, I hope, at least a little sweet.

PART ONE

The Elemental

1. Earth

Primitives see a great significance in contact with the earth, more than just an act of humility or subjection. . . . For the ground is seen as contact with the great mother to whom we shall all return. They do not see this as degrading or even humiliating, but simply a great joyful truth: the earth is our mother. We know that Christ also is of the earth, that he sprang from earth as man through Mary, and that he was buried in the earth in going down into death, but that he made this glorious and added a new significance and dimension to earthly life.

Matthew Kelty, "The Monastic Choir as Song and Dance,"
in Sermons in a Monastery, 33

❖ ❖ ❖ ❖ ❖

There are borders that do not appear on any maps. They mark territories, transitions, deep place, and deep space. I recall once hearing a professor from Venice, invited to lecture at a conference on "Mediterranean Studies," confess with a casual wave of his hand and a verbal flourish, that he did not know what "the Mediterranean" was, and he did not really know what "Europe" was either. Lord, I thought to myself, he's going to try to deconstruct this conference before it begins, like some pretentious Socratic gadfly. I was not as smart as I thought. For he continued, brilliantly. "These are fictions, of course. But this I do know," and here he paused, "in the Mediterranean we eat oil and drink wine. *Europe begins with butter and beer.*" There is deep truth in this. You will not find this truth on a map. True it is, nonetheless.[1]

Monastics are often drawn to landscapes that possess power. I think of the rolling hills and the long valley at Subiaco near Rome, where Saint Benedict initiated the vast tradition of western monasticism,[2] not far from where I am writing this now. Or of Mount Athos[3] on the Chalkidikean peninsula not far from Thessaloniki in Greece, the sacred heart of the Orthodox Christian world.

There is a hallowed stretch of ground in the central Kentucky hills roughly triangulated with Louisville and Lexington. It is stunning in its vast expanses and natural beauty—the rich soil here produces grass so vibrant it looks blue—and stunning still more for those it has produced. Abraham Lincoln (1809–1865)[4] was born here in a small cabin near the Sinking Spring

---

[1] I first learned this lesson from Lawrence Durrell, in this marvelous description of entering southern France: "Tournon, Valence, Montelimar and you are now in a new country, the kingdom of the olive and the cypress. Here the Mediterranean begins with its characteristic cuisine based on garlic and olive-oil, its concentration on herbs—saffron, thyme, fennel, sage, black pepper. Here, too, the aperitif changes to *pastis*—an aniseed drink which is a mild second cousin to the brain-storming northern Pernod. This, too, is the territory in which you make your first tentative exploration of the little rosé wines which are (with the famous exceptions like Tavel) hardly known abroad. Under the dusty glare of the Provençal sunlight this new diet seems supremely appropriate; appropriate too that the accents begin to change from chicken and mutton to fish—which comes to its apotheosis in the great *bouillabaisse* cauldrons of the port of Marseilles!" (Lawrence Durrell, "The River Rhone," in *Spirit of Place,* ed. Alan G. Thomas [New York: Marlow and Company, 1967], 330–31).

[2] See Matthew Kelty, "Saint Benedict's Day," in *My Song is of Mercy,* 101–4.

[3] For lovely reflection on this spiritual landscape, see Patrick Leigh Fermor, *The Broken Road: From the Iron Gates to Mount Athos,* ed. Colin Thurbon and Artemis Cooper (New York: New York Review Books, 2013), 269–349.

[4] For Father Matthew's reflections on Lincoln, another poetic writer produced by this same sacred soil, see "Three Wise Men," in *Sermons in a Monastery,* 114–18, as well as "Our Just Desserts?" and "Trust in God's Mercy," in *Singing for the Kingdom,* 41–44.

from which the area took its name. He grew up on a larger
working farm that the family rented close by Knob Creek. The
land is unusually well watered and vaguely reminiscent of the
Scottish Highlands. I'll come back to that.

The area received significant interest and attention from the
US Department of the Interior's Geological Surveyors, beginning in the late nineteenth century.[5] The more immediate area
near the Abbey of Gethsemani was studied closely by the US
Geological Survey, in cooperation with the Kentucky Geological Survey, between 1961 and 1978, the work beginning shortly
after Father Matthew joined the community.[6] Of particular
interest to them was a dramatic geological uplift that separates
Lincoln's Birth Home from the monastery, where an older
formation called the Silurian Rock outcrop has pushed up to
the surface precisely there. These findings were very helpfully
summarized by the National Park Service in 2010.[7] The report
is especially useful in that it provides an historical outline of
the regional findings from the Precambrian period (prior to
542 million years Before the Present [BP]), through the Paleo-
lithic (542–231 million years BP) to the Mesozoic (251 million
years BP to the present).

This region is an unusually dynamic one, in which a limestone and dolomite foundation has been covered by later,

---

[5] Henry Shaler Williams and Sir Edward M. Kindle, "Contributions to
Devonian Paleontology, 1903," Bulletin No. 244, Series C, *Systematic Geology
and Paleontology* 69 (Washington, DC: Government Printing Office, 1905).

[6] "Lithostratigraphy of the Silurian Rocks Exposed on the West Side of the
Cincinnati Arch in Kentucky," Geological Survey Professional Paper 1151-C
(Washington, DC: Government Printing Office, 1981).

Father Matthew knew something about this: "Time is such a frail, fragile
entity, so mysterious. A man picks up a stone on the road to the hill and tells
me it is probably two million years old! We are immersed in an eternity that
we are part of, alive in" ("A Lovely Flower Unfolding," in *Singing for the
Kingdom*, 118).

[7] "Abraham Lincoln's Birthplace National Historical Park: Geological Resources Inventory Report" (National Resource Report NPS/NRPC/GRD/
NRR-2010/219).

harder deposits. As the limestone deteriorated through chemical and sub-surface water erosion, an unstable system of caves, underwater pools, and sinkholes was created. The area near the Abbey of Gethsemani is the largest such system in the United States, and the nearby system of caves around Mammoth Cave National Park is the largest such system in the world. This has created a very unusual biosphere in which surface water is relatively rare, but the entire Pennyroyal Plateau is nestled atop a complex system of underground water filtered naturally through the porous stone. The so-called "karst" landscape (derived from a Slavic word, curiously, meaning "barren, stony ground") is thus nonetheless very close to water, which periodically breaks through to the surface in springs, pools, and occasional streams. It creates a rare, and unusual, and dynamic natural beauty, reminiscent (as I have said) of the Scottish Highlands.[8] Small wonder they turned the place to whiskey.

In point of fact, it is a land tailor-made for whiskey, for the planting of corn and soy and tobacco, as well as for the grazing of domestic herds. It was so in Lincoln's day, and it remains so today. "Knobs Creek" will be a familiar name to any bourbon drinker, but this small and distinctive piece of territory abounds with distilleries both small and large. Jim Beam is produced here, as is Makers Mark.[9] The weary wayfarer who stops in any tavern in this area, no matter how small or secluded or insignificant, will be treated to an impressive selection of distilled grains, served by a bartender who can tell you as much as you wish to know about each one. Pride in the

[8] In the Stone Age, the necessities for ancient peoples were caves for shelter, secure fresh water supplies, and hard stone (like quartz and chert) for tool-making; thus this area was ideal. It appears to have been inhabited, off and on, for at least 11,000 years.

[9] Both enterprises were recently purchased by a Japanese conglomerate for some sixteen billion dollars, with the promise that nothing in the production would change (apparently 40% of Makers Mark's production already ships to Japan).

production runs deep here. Neither butter nor beer, this place is defined by the bourbon.

It was here that a group of French Trappists decided to found the Abbey of Our Lady of Gethsemani in 1848.[10] More than forty choir and lay monks departed from their home—the Melleray Abbey, which was founded in 1145 and was located in the forbidding territories of the Loire Valley in Brittany—consisting of craftsmen in various trades and a few former soldiers (together with three aged "familiars" and two or-phans). While the vast majority were Frenchmen from nearby the abbey, the group included an Italian, an Irishman, a Span-iard, and a Swiss (thirteen more monks would be sent from Melleray to join them in 1851). They departed Melleray on the morning of October 24, 1848, marched on foot to Ancenis, took ship to Tours, then boarded a train for Paris; most had never seen a train before. The group then took ship at Le Havre, aboard *The Brunswick* bound for New Orleans. They left Le Havre on November 3, 1848, and, after arriving in New Or-leans, boarded the steamship *Martha Washington* for a ten-day cruise up the Mississippi and Ohio rivers, before landing finally in Louisville. After resting here for several days, the

---

[10] For a history of the founding of the Abbey of Gethsemani at its centen-nial, see Thomas Merton, *The Waters of Siloe* (New York: Harcourt, 1949), as well as the abbey's own publication, *Gethsemani Magnificat: Centenary of Geth-semani Abbey* (Trappist, KY: Gethsemani Publications, 1949).

A more recent study based upon the French archival evidence (primarily the *Annales* of Melleray Abbey and the *Memoirs* of Gethsemani's first abbot, Dom Eutropius), is Jay Butler, "From Melleray to Gethsemani: Spreading Cistercian Spirituality in the Early Nineteenth Century," *Cistercian Studies Quarterly* 53, no. 1 (2018): 73–95. Butler devotes his history to a close analysis of the serial irruptions of anti-clerical and anti-religious sentiment in the decades of the Revolution and Restoration in France. That the Melleray Abbey emerged from these cultural oscillations, managing not only to survive but actually to thrive, is what placed it in a position to seed Cistercian communi-ties such as Gethsemani (its first) in the New World. My historical summary in the next three paragraphs is indebted to, and derived from, Butler's superb essay. I am grateful to Marsha Dutton for this latter reference.

group left on foot again, arriving at Gethsemani in the late afternoon of December 21, 1848—the winter solstice.

The Melleray Abbey, like almost all monastic communities in France, had suffered terribly and repeatedly through the revolutionary paroxysms of the first half of the nineteenth century. The French Revolutionary Assembly dissolved all monastic orders, including the Cistercians, in 1790, though some monks stayed on at Melleray until 1792. It was then that its properties were pillaged and the lands sold at auction. Most of the monks fled either to England or to Switzerland; a large cohort of French transplants and English additions returned to Melleray in 1817, and within a decade they had far exceeded their former numbers and constituted the single largest Trappist monastery in France. After the 1830 revolution, the tide turned once again; Melleray was pillaged and depleted of its monks, but public reaction against the process was so severe that its fortunes were quickly restored. The decision to seed a new monastery was due primarily to the practical fact that Melleray had outgrown its capacity by the time of the 1848 revolution. Wary of committing new resources to the vagaries of various French regimes, the abbot, Dom Maxime, elected to send his monks to a more stable, and religiously friendlier, revolutionary republic: the United States.[11]

The oldest member of the party, Father Benezet, died on the Atlantic crossing at the age of seventy, a concrete and dramatic indication of the sacrifices to which all had been called. If one is inclined to tracing the influence of origins, then there is much about this voyage to consider closely. Observance at Melleray was strict and austere; the monks ate once a day and drank

---

[11] Dom Maxime mentioned a curious added feature for his decision in the *Annales.* Some American Catholics of abolitionist sympathies believed that a Trappist monastery at Gethsemani, displaying the virtues of manual labor, would inspire the local whites to take up such labor themselves, thereby creating the condition for the emancipation of their black slaves. See Butler, "From Melleray to Gethsemani," 92.

only water. But these transplant monks elected to add wine to their diet on the transatlantic crossing and shared the Loire Valley's largesse with other passengers, especially the nursing mothers. And so a new monastic tradition was born in the New World; it is hard not to recall Noah's cultivation of the grape in the aftermath of his long sea voyage, and the chaos that ensued. Abraham Lincoln was just twenty-nine years old at the time our stalwarts arrived in Kentucky, trying to make his way as a lawyer in Springfield, Illinois. One wonders what he would have made of the news. One may also wonder what the Vatican made of this news, the founding of a second men's monastic community in the United States in as many years.

Surprisingly, a thorough investigation of the Secret Archives at the Vatican Library turned up nothing regarding the founding of the Abbey of Gethsemani, just a precious few file folders containing correspondence about several loose and probably overlapping scandals. The first such file[12] contains a body of rather funny correspondence, beginning with a real gem, dated May 4, 1893, that is, less than fifty years from the Abbey's foundation.

Submitted by one Rev. B. Patrick, M.D., at the behest of the Abbot of Gethsemani, it informed the regional Church authorities that an experimental treatment (called the Keeley treatment) had been initiated at the Abbey a year earlier but had recently been suspended in order to be moved to a separate facility at Mt. Olivet, just one half-mile from the Abbey's grounds. Designed for what the Doctor quaintly refers to as "priests addicted to the liquor habit," the treatment consisted of four daily hypodermic injections, combined with oral supplements taken every two hours while the patient was awake, at the cost of one hundred dollars per patient for a treatment lasting four weeks in total. In the course of that month, the

---

[12] ASV: Delegazione apostolico / STATI UNITI D'AMERICA / IX. Louisville. 1 / Padri Trappisti di Gethsemani (1893 / 1901–1902 / 1906).

Doctor marveled, all appetite for liquor was banished by this treatment. Dr. Patrick indicated that he had delivered the treatment to twenty-five priests from Gethsemani in the last year (which would amount to roughly two priests per month), and that all but one of them had returned, almost miraculously, to their full duties. Hence, he opined, there was no remaining excuse for priests in the area to disgrace themselves and the religion they served. Based on the evidence of the remaining letters in this folder, whether excused or not, this problem persisted . . . with the predictable consequences for priests and local congregations, alike.

The five succeeding letters trace the travails of one Rev. John Lerman who was ousted from Gethsemani for excessive love of the bottle and who subsequently pleaded unsuccessfully for reinstatement. Father Matthew knew a thing or two about this history.

> Monks preach hospitality and practice it. Years ago, about a century, give or take a few years, the third floor east had private rooms reserved for priests who had drinking problems. Bishops would send them here for penance and reform for a month or two or longer. To be sure, we did nothing special for them in terms of their addiction. No one did in those days. Alcohol was thought a moral problem.[13]

So it was not necessarily the case that the carrying-on was by Gethsemani-based monks, at least not exclusively, so much as that Gethsemani was being used as a field hospital of sorts, in which and with which to reform any wayward priests in the region. Naturally, something special was being done for them, though Father Matthew (who was a great admirer of Alcoholics Anonymous) remained suspicious of the efficacy of moral cures for medical problems, like addiction.

[13] Matthew Kelty, "The Greatest of the Sacraments," in *Singing for the Kingdom*, 93.

The next two files[14] move from comedy[15] to tragedy: the first, outlining in some detail an eerily familiar case of sexual abuse involving the Principal of Gethsemane College, one Darnley Beaufort; and the second, a larger file concerning another wayward priest, one J. F. McSherry. McSherry, after serially abusing alcohol and several children in his care, appears to have appealed his case against the Bishop of Louisville to the Holy See, prompting a frustrated summary of the case by the Secretary of the Sacred Consistorial Court in Rome, who comments on the generally low and wayward quality of North American priests (*sacerdoti degenerati e scandalosi*, "degenerate and scandalous priests," were his words). Father Matthew was painfully aware of this problem, if not of this particular story, and attempted to turn it into a question of repentance rather than theodicy—on the whole in a less-than-fully convincing way.[16]

---

[14] Archivio della Delegazione Apostolica negli Stati Uniti. IX. Diocesi. Louisville (Kentucky) / Posiz. 15: Il Rev. B. M. Benedict; and Archivio della Delegazione Apostolica negli Stati Uniti. IX. Diocesi. Louisville (Kentucky) / Posiz. 18: Stato del Rev. J. F. McSherry, di Gethsemane. (1898–1904, 1911, 1916–1917).

[15] Comedy returns in Archivio della Delegazione Apostolica negli Stati Uniti. IX. Diocesi. Louisville (Kentucky) / Posiz. 47: Rev. F. X. Havelburg, di Trappist, ed il Vescovo (1909), in which a hapless Jewish convert, F. X. Havelburg, left the abbey and traveled to Rome to gain a hearing at the Holy See. Upon his return, he pleaded that he understood the apostolic delegate in Washington, DC, to have given him leave; the delegate gently but firmly demurred.

[16] I am thinking primarily of the following essentially moral observations: "One could say that Catholics deserve what they get in their priests, but the statement is gratuitous. The first twelve picked by Jesus give a good lesson. They were chosen by the Son of God. One of them was a disreputable man named Matthew. It would seem that more than appearances are involved. We really do not know much about the deeps of life." And again:

There are 50,000 victims of sexual abuse in Kentucky, according to a University of Kentucky poll a few years ago. Some of them became priests. Probably the past was never mentioned or noted, just a past hidden or denied, as is, or was, the usual approach. The great denial shared by our society. . . .

A last file (presumably written in 1923 and emended in 1930)[17] provides some general information about the Abbey of Gethsemani and the surrounding diocese. The diocese was founded in 1808 with its seat in Bardstown, before later being transferred to Louisville. Its first bishops were

Flaget: 1808–1841

Mons. Spalding: 1841–1865

Mons. Lavialle: 1865–1867

Mons. McCloskey: 1867–1909

Dionisio O'Donaghue: 1909– , but when he became infirm, an assistant (*Coadjutore*) was appointed: Mons. Giovanni Alessandro Floersh

---

Here comes my Irish superstition again. Are these guilty priests victims for the rest of us, expressions of God's displeasure at American morals or, if you will, American Catholic morals? Is the shortage of priests something we had coming, that we don't deserve them if we pay small heed to them?

Since I am troubled by these thoughts, I have to deal with them. . . . Can we read God into such tragic events as these? I don't think so. It is not that simple. Reading the mind of God is not that easy.

So instead of looking out, I look in. . . .

So the suffering of these priests does not so much make them victim souls immolated for themselves and all of us. Rather, they give us one more taste of the human scene. Our beautiful world and our beautiful people, not to say our beautiful children, are touched by the darkness of evil. Against that there is no hope save in the grace of God and the mercy of God.

("Our Just Desserts?" and "Trust in God's Mercy," both in *Singing for the Kingdom*, 42–44.) To conceive of alcoholism and sexual abuse as disease and disorder certainly does shift the moral register as Matthew wishes to do. But to assume that all such priests were victims in their turn, and to focus exclusively on their victimization, fails to address the need to break cycles of violence against self and other and misses entirely the extent of institutional cover-up. I must confess that I find these essays, especially the latter, among his most puzzling. They were published in 2008.

[17] Archivio della Delegazione Apostolica negli Stati Uniti. IX. Diocesi. Louisville (Kentucky) / Posiz. 70: Visita Apostolica (1923?, 1930).

The diocese is described as having fallen on hard times, with poor leadership, declining numbers, and declining income. In addition to the Abbey of Gethsemani (with its 118 monks and accompanying School), other Catholic orders included The Sisters of Charity of Nazareth, The Sisters of Loretto at the Foot of the Cross, The Dominican Sisters of Mercy, a Catholic Hospital (led by three Sisters' organizations, Franciscan and other), and two groups of Ursuline Sisters with 600 members. It was the Sisters of Loretto, incidentally, who had acquired the land upon which the Abbey of Gethsemani was eventually to be built.

Most of the Catholics in this area were Irish and German, with some few Italians and, significantly, three African American communities.[18] In November 1928, one Matthew O'Doherty died, leaving $4 million in his estate, some $2 million of which he left to the Catholic diocese. When the family contested the will, a compromise was reached, requiring the Church to return $725,000. But most of the gift had been in stocks and real estate, and by 1930, their value had plummeted. The diocese managed, through Bishop Floersh's ministrations, to take out a loan to manage the payment.

Thirty years later, when Father Matthew Kelty joined this community, the Abbey of Gethsemani and the diocese were very different places. And the place continued to change through his very long, if episodic, tenure there.[19] The presence of Thomas Merton (1915–1968) had something to do with that. Not only did Father Louis (the name Merton was given) serve

[18] Toni Morrison has done much to remind her American readership that the Catholic Church had a far better record than its Protestant rivals in defending the rights of all peoples and promoting abolition in the United States; she converted to Catholicism at the age of twelve. For some striking reflection on this issue, see Toni Morrison, *A Mercy* (New York: Alfred A. Knopf, 2008).

[19] A new book, Michael Casey and Clyde F. Crews, *Monks Road: Gethsemani into the Twenty-First Century* (Collegeville, MN: Liturgical Press, 2016), tells this story beautifully in essays and photographs.

as Father Matthew's novice master when he first joined the community,[20] but Father Matthew served as Merton's confessor in his last year at the monastery. Merton eventually convinced the abbot, Dom James, that the eremitic life was in fact compatible with Cistercian tradition, and thereafter lived more peripherally on the grounds of the abbey.[21] That same abbot followed suit when he stepped down,[22] and even Father Matthew maintained three small retreats in his long life at the monastery. Merton also made the Abbey of Gethsemani famous through his voluminous correspondence, the endless range of visitors, and, most of all, his published books. As time went on, the Abbey was quietly transformed into an intentional community that puts a premium on the fine arts.[23] Father Matthew was an important contributing member to that change as well, in his homilies and in print.

So this place has a history, as well as a spirituality and stunning physical landscape. But we must go deeper, as Father Matthew was fond of saying—quite literally, in this case. The US Geological surveys have revealed the presence of massive amounts of fossilized deposits in virtually every layer of the region—primarily crinoids, brachyopods, bryozoans, corals, and, later, small marine animals such as trilobytes. In the Paleozoic period, when scientists believe the world consisted primarily of one enormous landmass ("Pangea"), this place was underwater. It was a part of the so-called Iapetos Ocean,

[20] See "Flute Solo," in *My Song is of Mercy*, 10–14, where Matthew recalls this period as an "ordeal."

[21] Matthew Kelty, "On Dom James," in *My Song is of Mercy*, 122–23.

[22] For Merton's own rather ironic view of the matter, see his final journal, *The Other Side of the Mountain*, ed. Patrick Hart (New York: HarperCollins Publishers, 1998), 36, 46.

[23] See Father Matthew's reflections on the role that the monk Lavrans, an icon painter of exceptional vision and rare artistry, played in this development before his departure from the Abbey of Gethsemani in 1976 (*My Song is of Mercy*, 225–28).

which later, when the African and American continents slowly pulled apart, was to become the Atlantic Ocean.

In other words before the place was Earth, it was Water.

2. Water

Though a son of the Archer and linked to fire, it is to
water that I have a more natural leaning. Water is always
an invitation to immersion, an immersion with a quality
of totality, since it would accept all of me, as I am.
Some primal urge invites me to return whence I came.

Matthew Kelty, "Flute Solo," in *My Song is of Mercy*, 65

There is no denying that the sea is a good metaphor of
God. Its majesty and power stagger the mind of human
beings. For the most part, the voyage was one of fair,
mild weather, yet anyone who knows the Pacific knows
its gift for violence and treachery. The sea can be cruel,
relentless, without remorse or regret.

God is strangely like the sea. His ways are beyond
fathoming, as was said long ago.

Matthew Kelty, "Flute Solo," in *My Song is of Mercy*, 27

❖ ❖ ❖ ❖ ❖

In the beginning, there was water. This is what the first
creation account in the book of Genesis declares. God's
spirit hovered over it, though it lacked form, until God formed it,
then formed land masses, then created life to dwell within and
without. One of the more striking aspects of Christian orthodoxy is thus the doctrine of God's creation *ex nihilo*, "out of
nothing." For there was something, there was material stuff;

it simply lacked form. And this primal stuff bore a name: "the waters." Matthew would often refer to this as "the deeps."

Gary Wills makes an interesting observation about Augustine: he only encountered water twice in his life.[1] The first time was when he left North Africa for Rome to begin his training and his eventual, tumultuous trajectory into the Christian community. The second was his return trip from the Roman port at Ostia, where his beloved mother Monica died, followed by his subsequent return to Hippo Regium and his long career as pastor, as writer, and as bishop. The imagery to which he gravitated in meditating on the divine presence involved mountains, not seas. This may have made him an especially sensitive reader of the Psalms, an altogether mountainous spiritual meditation on God,[2] but it left him somewhat at sea when it came to more fluid matters. In other words, this definitive doctor of the Western churches had no real feel for water.

Charles Sprawson has written a truly remarkable meditation on what he calls "the feeling for water" (as well as, he adds, "the psychology of the swimmer"). That book, *Haunts of the Black Masseur*,[3] may also be read as a cultural history of recreational swimming, and is the product of a very personal and deeply Romantic obsession. Sprawson observes that the Classical Greeks swam in streams, rivers, and seas and that they peopled all of these water sources with divinity, the liquid anima that so inspired their mythic reveries:

> For the Greeks water possessed magical, mysterious, and often sinister properties. There was a spring that made you mad, another that once tasted could make you teetotal for the rest of your life. In another Hera renewed her virginity

[1] Gary Wills, *Saint Augustine* (New York: Penguin Putnam, Inc., 1999), 1–2.

[2] Peter Brown, *Augustine of Hippo: A Biography* (Berkeley, CA: University of California Press, 1967, 2000), 121–24, 151–75, 271–78, 436, 449–51.

[3] Charles Sprawson, *Haunts of the Black Masseur: The Swimmer as Hero* (New York: Pantheon, 1994).

every year. . . . Water caused men to fall in love with their reflections, reduced them to hermaphrodites, those indeterminate figures of androgynous beauty that haunted their artistic imagination. The Styx in Arcadia inflicted death on men and animals, dissolved glass, crystal, stone, corrupted metal, even gold. . . .

Greek civilisation seemed to revolve around water. The great battles with the Persians were fought near famous springs. When Lysander, the Spartan commander, was killed below the walls of Haliartus, the historian cannot help interrupting his narrative in adding that he was positioned "near the spring called Cissusa, where the infant Dionysus, according to legend, was washed by his nurses after his birth; at any rate the water had something of the colour and sparkle of wine, and is clean and very sweet to drink." . . . It was common for Olympic champions to be buried near frontier rivers, as was Koroibos, the Elean who won the first race in the Olympic Games. The Games themselves were held by famous springs or rivers, whose water flowed round the courses and among the spectators. For the lyric poet Pindar the grace of athletic movement seemed like pure water running over sand. . . . Socrates conducted his discourse on the nature of love and beauty in the *Phaedrus*, by a spring "most lovely" that flowed under them, whose water was "very cool, to judge by my foot, and the figurines and statues seem to designate it as a sacred place of some nymph and of Achelous." The once sacred stream of Ilissus now flows underground through the drains of Athens, and eventually trickles into the Kephisos before reaching the sea in a marsh which provided Byron with the woodcock he ate for lunch. 200 years ago Athens was still watered by fourteen public fountains supplied by the ancient aqueducts.[4]

The Romans, by contrast, swam in more controlled water environments; two of the defining symbols of the Roman imperium are aqueducts and bath complexes, after all:

[4] Sprawson, *Haunts of the Black Masseur*, 53–56.

The element that to the Greeks seemed so mysterious and fugitive, the Romans attempted to control. They perfected the umbrella. Their hours were marked by the drip of water clocks, *horologia ex aqua*, which became in time sought-after status symbols, so ingenious and elaborate that automatic floats struck the hour by tossing eggs or pebbles into the air. Byron alludes to Roman water "imprisoned" in marble, and the enshrined water in fountains and swimming pools made of glacial marble and other forms of stone quarried from all corners of the Empire, the purple-streaked Phrygian, the green-speckled Laconian, and from Gythion, stones shaped like river pebbles. The Greeks had built only one pool, in Olympia, and their swimming, except for the Spartans in the Eurotas, was mostly mythical or ritual. "Three things reveal the magnificence of Rome," records a historian from Halicarnassus, "the aqueducts, the roads, and the sewers." Long, arched aqueducts conveyed over 200 million gallons of water a day into the city of Rome.[5]

But, and here is the key, the early Christians turned decisively away from the water, in Sprawson's view:

> After Rome's fall water gradually lost its allure. . . . With the coming of Christianity the West began to lose interest in the sea and the tradition that had spread gradually from Greece and the Aegean. All along the Mediterranean coast villages that had once looked on the sea turned their energies inland. A maritime civilization turned into one devoted to land, and Islam took possession of the Mediterranean. Of the 400 steam baths built by the Moors among the fountains of Granada only one survived the first hundred years of Christianity.
>
> The church filled the sea with fantastic and imaginary monsters. . . .
>
> The status of the swimmer gradually declined. No longer was he a hero, capable like the Nordic Beowulf of exploits

---

[5] Sprawson, *Haunts of the Black Masseur*, 59.

beyond human capability. Now he needed supernatural intervention to survive. . . .

Swimming, like sexual pleasure, came to be associated somehow with the devil, and was almost suppressed during the domination of Europe by Christianity. It was not until the beginning of the nineteenth century that its popularity revived.[6]

Peopling the deep with monsters that recall Leviathan and Behemoth, the Christians turned away from the ocean, not to return until the nineteenth century. When they did so return— and we may think of Goethe's swims during his Italian Journey, or Byron's legendary crossing of the Hellespont, Shelley's bizarre drowning off La Spezia, and so on—the Romantics swam in order to reclaim and restore the ancient, pagan feel for water:

> When, in a mood of spiritual desolation, Romantics of the nineteenth century were to lament the loss to modern man of that Greek mythopoetic view of the world, that enabled them to humanise the natural scene and feel at home in the universe, it was to the deities of their waters that they turned in despair. It was their absence that they felt most strongly, through them that they expressed their disgust with contemporary life.[7]

These Romantics, many of them at any rate, thought that the Christian culture of Europe was dying. The question for them thus became how to breathe new life into dying sacred institutions, or else how to dispense with those institutions altogether. "Going back to the *Greeks*" was a trajectory charted out by a great many disaffected Romantics. But in "going back to Greece," the question of where, and when, we are going emerged with dramatic urgency. It is both an archaeological

---

[6] Sprawson, *Haunts of the Black Masseur*, 67–69.
[7] Sprawson, *Haunts of the Black Masseur*, 56–57.

and an historical question, a question ultimately of *origins*. Go back to a certain epoch—the third or fourth century, let us imagine—and you travel back to a certain kind of Christianity, *Orthodox* Christianity, which represented the road not taken in the Latin West. Go back further still, and you leave Christianity altogether, returning to Father Matthew's beloved Celts. Many Romantics went there, back to the pagan, pre-Christian world and the feeling for myth (and water) we moderns have allegedly lost. Goethe and Shelley and Byron all flirted with this pagan idea (Nietzsche would be more emphatic)—and what they discovered was another sort of religion altogether, an alternative kind of spirituality, one that might also be the very palliative we need in the face of an incomplete Christian premise or promise.

These Romantics also swam naked. And so did Father Matthew. I will come back to that issue several times here, since it raises a fundamental question of sensuality and sexuality, and of their necessary relation, which much preoccupies this good monk. But first there seems to be something off kilter in Sprawson's historical narrative, an interpretive problem we need to address. The early Christians, actually, seem rather *drawn* to the water. Baptism was one of their central ritual events, seemingly from the outset. John reports that Jesus claimed to offer "the water of life," which, once received, would alleviate all future thirst. And the Church was often depicted as a ship, reminiscent of Noah's Ark.

When Father Matthew departed from the Abbey of Gethsemani for his nine-year sojourn in solitude at Papua New Guinea, he describes a formative experience that inspired his first reverie upon this Christian imagery of and aboard ship, en route to his hermit's final Melanesian destination:

> The ship was much like a monastery. There was good enclosure, better than the best cloister walls. The captain made a worthy abbot, nor was a prior wanting, a subprior. Obedience was evident in practice, devotion to duty, to labor.

The ship was no less a journey than any monastery, and the presence of God was not subtle. True, there was no explicit praise of God, as one finds in every group of monks, yet his praise was there and I heard it. People of the sea live close to God. . . .

Some think monasteries unusual and artificial. Rather, I find them as common and natural as a Greyhound bus crossing Kansas, or a subway crossing town, not to say a ship at sea.[8]

He returned to this same, staggering insight twenty-five years later, back home at the monastery, while still enjoying temporary periods of solitary life:

I was reminded of that just last week when a blustery wind was whipping those huge sheets of plastic that sheathe the side of the retreat house against rain, sounding for all the world like sails snapping loose and wild as we change course.

We are much a ship. And we are in it together. We certainly could not trip alone. I know, I tried it. And we need everyone on board. Who could we spare? Name him. We need all, can spare none. Every single one. If he is not here, it is not Gethsemani. If you are not here, it is some other place, some other time. The infinitely complex web of divine genius that led us all here is only the beginning of a mysterious love that keeps us here, treasures us, loves us, delights in us.[9]

The big thing, of course, in Father Matthew's view, is the Church. And the Church is a profound after-echo of Noah's original, saving ark. And yet there is a further, a more subtle

---

[8] Kelty, "Flute Solo," in *My Song is of Mercy*, 25.

[9] Kelty, "Flute Solo," 157. He continues: "For we are so few. The ship so small. The sea so huge. What are 12 monasteries but one small fragment of Catholic America, not to say whole America? And even in the Church, we are a modest Order. In the world at large so trifling. Procter and Gamble soap a bigger enterprise."

complexity here. As Joseph Conrad famously observed,[10] sailors do not love the sea; quite the opposite in fact. They fear her. What they love are ships, ships that ideally protect them from the sea's vast and terrible danger.

Swimmers, of course, are another matter; they love the water. And Father Matthew appears to have loved it immoderately, in all its forms. As rain:

> No rain falls that I do not at once hear in the sound of the falling water an invitation to come to the wedding. It is rare that I do not answer. A walk in an evening rain in any setting is to walk in the midst of God's loving attention to his earth, *and like a baptism*, is not simple washing, but a communication of life. When you hurry in out of the rain, I hurry out into it, for it is a sign that all is well, that God loves, that good is to follow.[11]

As snow:

> When rain turns to ice and snow, I declare a holiday. I could as easily resist as stay at a desk with a parade going by in the street below. I cannot hide the delight that then possesses my heart. Only God could have surprised rain with such a change of dress as ice and snow. . . . Snow charms all young hearts. Only when you get older and bones begin to feel dampness, when snow becomes a traffic problem and a burden in the driveway, when wet means dirt—then poetry takes flight and God's love play is not noted. . . .
>
> Bright wintry mornings the temperature would sometimes drop to zero around Gethsemani. When there would be deep snow I would take off to the woods, if the chance came. . . . When it was really cold I used to strip quickly and roll in the snow for a bit. In no time the body would react, heat up almost instantly, and one would stand, looking at the brilliant blue above, steam rising from all over one's

[10] Joseph Conrad, *The Mirror of the Sea* (New York: Harper & Brothers, 1906), 122–23.

[11] Kelty, "Flute Solo," 65–66, italics mine.

glistening flesh. One did not wait too long and push it beyond its time, but dress wet as fast as one could. *It was a wintry baptism and good for the soul.*[12]

As dew:

> When I had that happy house beside the lake at Gethsemani, I had to walk through summer fields to reach it. Sometimes it was so rich an experience that I began to suspect it was sinful. The path crossed a small hill, descended through a wooded grove, then over the bottom of a long meadow. Mornings, the tall grass would be leaning over the path with dew, all sprinkled with truly thousands of diamonds so large you could see a rainbow in each. The wood to the left was blued with mist, and inside was cool darkness. I would be wet almost to the waist with such a freshness that I wondered if a shower of dew would not be a remarkable sort. Yet, by the time I would be heading back to the abbey, the sun would be up in the sky, the dew gone, the grass dry, the mist lifted, the woods patterned in sharp light and shadow. Then I would say to myself that I should not get so carried away with passing things.[13]

Each of these passages comes from a portion of *Flute Solo* entitled "Primal Water" (one that began with his identification as a "son of the Archer"), but this last image is especially striking, not just for the intense sensuality of the description, and the whole experience, but for the cautious worry he expresses in 1973—that this, his own poetic and luxuriating sensuality, may be excessive. A sign of sin, not a baptism from sin. At some point and in some way, Father Matthew must have worked all that out. For when asked later in life why he had become a monk, he simply quipped, "Somebody has to walk in the rain!"[14]

---

[12] Kelty, "Flute Solo," 66–67, italics mine.

[13] Kelty, "Flute Solo," 67.

[14] Matthew Kelty, *Singing for the Kingdom: The Last of the Homilies*, MW 15 (Kalamazoo, MI: Cistercian Publications, 2008), ix.

He reveled in bodies of water of all sorts, the more isolated the better:

> My hermitage in the wood is the old pump house by Dom Frederic's lake. The little house is at the bottom of the cement dam which holds back the water in a deep gorge and forms a relatively large lake. The pump house has the valves and at one time had the pumps to help the water over to the monastery and up into the water tower. So I took over the little house, about twelve feet by eight feet and ideal. Back of me, then, and above is the lake, large and beautiful and surrounded by woods. In front of me is a little pool where some run-off water gathers and where cows used to drink years ago. It is small, very deep and full of rotten matter. I call it "compunction pool", just as the other is the "joyous lake." It is there in front of me to look at. It is very lovely and is shaded over in summer with trees and vines. But it is black and deep and full of mystery.
>
> I have stripped and plunged into it a few times and come out covered with a black dye from the boggy matter. Then I ran up to the joyous lake and washed it away. I think we need to plunge into our own depths like that now and again. We need this contact with darkness.[15]

We should consider this passage closely; it is typical of Father's Matthew's prose: simple, elemental even, but gesturing at great depth. In short order we learn that he, too, took up in a hermitage of sorts, a converted pump house in this case (he had three of them).[16] Even here in the monastery, he was drawn to water (doubtless it was in this way that he could

---

[15] Kelty, "The Dinner Party," in *Sermons in a Monastery*, 95–96.

[16] Brother Paul Quenon, in his recently published memoir, devotes an entire chapter to the Merton-inspired hermitages of the Abbey of Gethsemani. See "Our Golden Age of Hermitages," in *In Praise of the Useless Life: A Monk's Memoir* (Notre Dame, IN: Ave Maria Press, 2018), 61–78. Father Matthew's experience of hermitage life at Gethsemani is described at 73–74. I am deeply indebted to Brother Paul for sharing this with me, and for so very much else besides.

recall his earlier periods as a solitary in Papua New Guinea). The hermitage fronted directly onto two bodies of water, divided by a cement dam that recalls God's first actions in Genesis: separating the waters. Very near to Father Matthew's hermitage, the lake was large and crystalline; the pond was far smaller, rank and rotten. Yet Father Matthew chose to swim in both. Peeling off his clothes, he would intentionally dirty himself with compunction, then cleanse himself with joy, emerging from his ablutions cleansed, refreshed, made new. Father Matthew wrote this meditation in Thomas Merton's hermitage, he informs us, and he uses it as an occasion to reflect upon the power of evil, on the reality of angels and demons or, at the very least, of the angelic and demonic capacity in all people, even and especially monastic people. His reflections on water's benediction are overshadowed, clouded over, by this damnable question of evil.

That Father Matthew did all of this bathing naked is also noteworthy. Nudity has many registers: from sensuality and eroticism, to the innocence of childhood or Eden. In this passage, Father Matthew plays subtly with imagery and emotions borrowed from the Genesis account of God's various creations— first of the bodies of water, and then of the Man. Adam and the Woman (it is noteworthy she does not get a name, Hava, until they have both been expelled) were originally naked in Eden, and they were utterly unashamed of that fact. Innocent. The first sign that something has gone amiss is the shame they feel in the face of their own (and perhaps one another's) nudity; they fashion a primitive covering for themselves and this is how God learns what has transpired. Cloaked nudity as lost innocence. And yet we see Father Matthew happily returning to such innocence, Pooh-like, peeling off his clothes in all seasons, reveling in the feeling of his own body glistening in the summer sun, or steaming in the grey clouds of winter. This is "flute solo"; this is skin and embodiment. And it is good.

The whole thrust of Father Matthew's meditations on water concerns baptism of various kinds as the restoration of a lost innocence, a restored relation to divine principle. Thomas Merton describes similarly transgressive bodily play in his later journals, though his body was drawn more to sunlight than to water. He was trying to find en*light*enment, whereas Father Matthew's lifelong quest was for mercy. For this one may need the water. There is an intense fluidity to human life, after all, and this is as much a matter of time and of history as of our evolutionary origins in the deep.[17] In other words, the deeps were a spiritual, as well as elemental, terrain in Father Matthew's experience.

What this playful, naked monk came to see was that we are all unique (as created by God), and all immortal (as loved by our Creator), and to know this deeply is to feel the embrace of water. And yet—here is the agonizing afterword—as the early church fathers were forced to acknowledge very early on, the ritual of baptism does not resolve evil, and does not render embodied, time-bound souls immune to their sinful double-dealing. Anything but that—compunction endures. Evil was to be the perennial problem of the water spirit now confined to the land.

[17] For a fascinating account of the call of deep water, one that begins with the relatively new sport of free-diving and ends with new experimental evidence that organic life originated under the intense pressure of deep water near sulphurous, volcanic vents, see James Nestor, *Deep: Freediving, Renegade Science, and What the Oceans Tell us about Ourselves* (New York: Houghton Mifflin Harcourt, 2014), 204–11. I have reflected further on these themes in "Names 'Writ on Water': Liquidity under Pressure," *liquid blackness* (forthcoming).

3. Fire

There must be an element of madness in our life. However, in saying this, one must make some distinctions.

Matthew Kelty,
"There Must Be an Element of Madness in our Life,"
from *Sermons in a Monastery*, 14

❖ ❖ ❖ ❖ ❖

It is a jarring story with which to begin a Sunday homily
(this was on March 4, 1990), but Father Matthew was nothing
if not jarring at times:

> Some months ago, an unfortunate Kentucky man named
> Mahoney drove down a throughway on the wrong side—
> being drunk—and ran head-on into a busload of young
> people. A terrible tragedy. Later, at the time of his trial, I
> asked one or the other of the monks, of people I ran into,
> what they would recommend if they were on the jury. The
> answers were a mix: one suggested the death penalty, an-
> other—and he a long-time prison chaplain—that the man
> be given a life sentence, another three years in prison and
> lifelong abstinence from alcohol, another that what he actu-
> ally got (an extensive prison sentence) was about the best
> you could do. I myself thought that a fitting sentence would
> be his visiting every high school in Kentucky and talking to
> the students about drunk driving. That would be of some
> use to him and to others. Even if the state paid him, it would

be cheaper and more effective as therapy and penance than prison would be.[1]

This prompts Father Matthew to an equally jarring reflection on how monastic communities served as models for the earliest North American penitentiaries. But the moral of his story is, well, moral in a way:

> These people I have spoken of, from Mahoney on down, are not wicked people. They are unfortunate. Poor. Weak. And confused. Misled. Quite unknowingly. . . . So we turn to compunction of heart lest we run into tragedy over the hill. Lent is time for tears over the human condition. Yours. Mine, Everyone's.[2]

Aristotle observed that the virtuous person, in this case the just man, can do unjust things.[3] In other words, the moral life is not constituted by a checklist; it is not about rules, laws, and regulations. Ethics, like virtue itself, is a more malleable, more supple, and more forgiving concept than that. As was the Christian faith, in Father Matthew's understanding of the central matter of grace and mercy.

When Father Matthew returned from his first sojourn in Papua New Guinea (1947–1951), he was assigned to the Society of the Divine Word's Illinois offices as editor of their magazine, *The Christian Family*. It was there, just as he was preparing to leave that assignment and join the Abbey of Gethsemani, that he may have burned down the publishing house:

> I was getting ready to go, delayed only by previously arranged engagements for some sisters' retreats, when the fire broke out in the press. It was a shocking experience and only emphasized what I had already sensed of the dramatic

[1] Matthew Kelty, "Mockery," in *My Song is of Mercy*, 189.
[2] Kelty, "Mockery," 191.
[3] Aristotle, *Nicomachean Ethics* 1134a16, 1136a25–30.

moment in that period of my life. I injured my foot badly on hot asphalt in escaping from the burning building and it took a while to heal. While the wound was still serious I gave one retreat in Dayton and a second to some novices in northern Wisconsin. While returning from the latter I had another taste of death. The train was racing toward Chicago bright and early that sunny wintry morning, still in the country, when it struck a large truck at a remote crossing. When the train finally stopped and backed up to the scene of the accident, they came to the diner and brought me out into the bitter cold and bitter sight of three bodies flung around the snow and under the twisted wreck. I could smell death and blood while I held one young man in my arms as he went into eternity. The second was a blond young boy in leather boots and leather jacket. I baptized him with melted snow. The third was dead. A long while later an ambulance came and took them away; we got back into the train and went on our way. When we left the train in Chicago I saw the damage done to the front of the locomotive; I felt a worse damage and knew in my heart that I was more afraid of God than ever, and remembered cold blood on the snow. A few days later I left on a night train for Louisville. The evening before we had a social evening in the priests' recreation room and I had all I could get to drink.[4]

This is one of the strangest, and also one of the most ominous, passages in the entire corpus of Father Matthew's writings. He tells us simply that "the fire broke out in the press," but he does not tell us how, nor where he was, nor how his feet came to be scalded on burning asphalt. Furthermore, what in the world must it have been like, this transition from dining car to death-hewn snowbank? And how in the world did this traumatized younger monk feel getting aboard another train just three days later—three days, that is, the time bridging crucifixion and resurrection, time's suspension in the face of

---

[4] Kelty, "Flute Solo," in *My Song is of Mercy*, 9–10.

eternity—a train taking him, moreover, off to his new fate: the Abbey of Our Lady of Gethsemani?

It is also striking that Father Matthew's primary emotional response to all of this was fear, the fear of God. We know the old adage, that such fear may be "the beginning of wisdom." But that does not seem to be how Father Matthew experienced his fear then. Not at all; he needed a stiff drink. Some years later, he was to preach a stirring sermon both relevant to and illuminating of this experience—on the *hatred* of God:

> I do not see how any progress at all can be made until we see how hate stems from a basic hatred of God. We sense that God does not love us, for obvious reasons, and so we respond by not loving God, by hating God. And since we cannot hate God who is pure spirit, we hate whatever is capable of receiving that hate, the Church or any of God's creatures. I do not see how we can move one inch further along the road to love and the abandonment of hatred until we acknowledge the presence of this hatred for God in us.[5]

The flip side of hatred is mercy, a crucial example of which is forgiveness. Father Matthew returned repeatedly to this, his central insight about mercy: namely, that it is a form of forgiveness in three dimensions: "forgiveness of God; forgiveness of our neighbor; forgiveness of ourselves."[6] All we can say with certainty is that Father Matthew's world, at least at this troubled juncture in his professional and personal life, was often a world of blood and fire. Forgiving himself, and his God, took a long time and enormous spiritual effort:

> My first encounter with death as a priest was with a young man burned in a grass fire while the men in his village were hunting pigs. They surrounded the pigs with fire and then speared them when they would dart free. He got caught in

[5] Kelty, "Hatred of God," in *The Call of Wild Geese*, 88–89.
[6] Kelty, "Forgiveness," in *The Call of Wild Geese*, 42ff.

a wind change and all his skin was burned from his body except for his face. He was past pain because his nerves were burned away. I baptized him and anointed him.[7]

At this stage, it—the way God's burning world was made—terrified and angered him. Baptized by fire quite literally, this is how Father Matthew made his way to the monastery. The 1960s were just getting underway.

It was a fire-y and an apocalyptic time. One thinks of the Vietnam War, the carpet bombing and napalm. One thinks of the Cold War and the nearly continuous reflection on nuclear Armageddon—"mutual assured destruction," in the sad parlance of diplomacy. Closer to home, one thinks of the Civil Rights movement, the profound political response to black bodies hanged and burned in the era of Jim and Jane Crow, of street protests and of protestors gunned down in those same streets, of extensive riots, Molotov cocktails, blind rage, entire cities gutted. Those times can seem almost eerily like our own.

An entry from Thomas Merton's last journal captures the terror of this cultural moment very well. It is dated March 20, 1968:

> Incredible things in the news. New laws (in New York) permitting police to shoot to kill if they even *suspect* someone might be carrying a weapon. Or if they resist arrest! Rumors of prison camps being prepared for the summer rioters (probably with some basis of truth). Utter corruption and hopelessness of South Vietnam, where the Americans are really being *beaten*—but where they may resort to tactical nuclear weapons. A sudden (late) awakening of Congress to the gravity of the situation, the lies they have believed (Tonkin Gulf incident, Pueblo incident), the mistakes they have made. Even the general public is perhaps beginning to get some idea of the enormous wrong that has been done

[7] Matthew Kelty, "Our Names are Written in Heaven," in *Singing for the Kingdom*, 124.

by the Johnson administration. The country itself is almost on the verge of economic crisis. One gets the sense that suddenly everyone—including business (*Wall Street Journal*, etc.)—is waking up and trying to prevent a disaster before it is too late.

I have never had such a feeling of the strange madness that possesses this country. And yet there is still some hope—not based on reason but on a basic good will and a luck that might still hold. Or is there a basic good will? Has it all been mortgaged to a police state? Are we already *there*? We may be![8]

Within several months, Dr. Martin Luther King Jr. and Robert Kennedy had both been assassinated, President Johnson announced that he would not seek a second term as US President, the Democratic Convention exploded in Chicago, and Richard Nixon was elected to the White House. The times were not a-changin'.

In that same meditation on evil that Father Matthew penned at Thomas Merton's hermitage, he finds himself reading Camus, to whom Merton had first introduced him:

I have been living with Camus these last few days and am haunted by the mystery of sin. When I was in the library I saw a few photos of the Viet Nam war and some items in *The Critic* of priests in vestments being taken by the police. I regret that I do not keep up with the news and with events. I should and encourage the juniors to do so, but I do not find the time and you cannot do everything. But the war and the chaos of our own time does not escape me.[9]

Perhaps. These Gethsemani monks, some of them at any rate, who have the gift of undistracted (though decidedly not

[8] Thomas Merton, *The Other Side of the Mountain*, ed. Patrick Hart (New York: HarperCollins, 2010), 69–70.

[9] Matthew Kelty, "The Dinner Party," in *Sermons in a Monastery*, 91.

unstructured) time suited to long meditation, know more about the comings and goings of this mad, bad world of ours than Father Matthew lets on. In a rhapsodic appreciation of Bob Dylan, whom Father Matthew called "a young poet" as well as a musician, he offers the following parallelism:

> The hippie movement may have developed because monks were not doing what they were called to do. There is some-thing poignant about it. Though we may shake our grey heads over dope and dirt and debauchery, there was more to it than that. We believe in love, do we not? Is not love the most important thing in the world to us? . . . We too are flower children. Perhaps the hippie movement was a sting-ing rebuke to us that we are not getting through, perhaps a word of encouragement to us. How great must be the need for the kind of thing we are trying to do if the very children cry out for it![10]

Imagine that: Flower Power as a call to reform of North America monasticism. It takes the creative eye and ear of someone like Father Matthew to sniff out that connection. And so he did.

He had help, of course, and one suspects that a great deal of help came from Thomas Merton. Merton's journals, his vo-luminous correspondence and his essaying, all demonstrate a profound level of engagement with current events. Father Matthew shared Merton's taste for the new music of the 1960s, the new poetry, the avant-garde. They both sympathized with the cultural youth movements that provided, at a minimum, an important symptomatology of the North America psyche. Faced with fire, Merton turned to the east, Matthew to the water. Merton died in this fire.

Thomas Merton, who had gone to Bangkok to deliver a lecture (on Marxism and Monasticism) at a conference dedi-cated to comparative monasticism, concluded his public ad-

---

[10] Matthew Kelty, "Desolation Row," in *Sermons in a Monastery*, 24–25.

dress by saying, rather elliptically, "And now I will disappear."
He returned to his bungalow after lunch and apparently died
due to heart attack, electrocution by faulty wiring from the
standing fan in his room, or both. Through the years, some
have repeatedly expressed the suspicion that Merton was mur-
dered.[11] His death was discovered some time after and his
body, with the fan still operating atop his corpse, was slightly
burned, though to what degree is uncertain. Merton's corpse
was returned to the United States, ironically enough, in a US
military plane bearing American casualties home from Vietnam;
it was indeed an age of burning, of napalm, of fire.[12] Merton's
funeral at Gethsemani was unusual, among other things, in
that the body was not made available for viewing.

> The coffin was not opened so it turned out that I was right
> when I saw him leave and said to myself, "We'll never see
> him again."
> Father John Eudes, our own medical doctor, looked at him
> in Louisville. Father Louis is the only one buried in a coffin
> in our cemetery that I know of, which is like him! The coffin

[11] The case has been made most forcefully by Hugh Turley and David
Martin, *The Martyrdom of Thomas Merton: An Investigation* (Hyattsville, MD:
McCabe Publishing, 2018). The book lays out the primary anomalies in the
case, perhaps most notably the absence of an autopsy, inattention to the
bleeding wound at the back of the head, the swiftness with which the US
Embassy took control of the body and arranged for its transport home, and
the apparent suppression of two photographs taken by Father Celestine Say
at the scene as soon as Merton's body was discovered. What is less convincing is their apparent assumption that the story of the faulty fan and Merton's
electrocution amounts to rendering his death meaningless and, even worse,
assigns the blame for Merton's death to his own clumsiness. I also do not see
that the evidence they assemble suggests a cover-up by the Abbey of Gethsemani. Nonetheless, the book raises important questions that warrant further
discussion. Of added interest is Paul Quenon's "Merton's Death as Seen From
the Home Grounds," in *In Praise of the Useless Life*, 109–18; Quenon makes
much of the metaphor of burning, as I do, at 116.

[12] See Patrick Hart's somber remarks in *The Other Side of the Mountain*,
xviii–xix.

was one of those typical monsters you would think were turned out in the shops of Metro-Goldwyn-Mayer. The readings from the Book of Jonah in the Mass were appropriate. There was a whale in front of us with Father Louis inside.

Father Dan Walsh, who was the man's first link to Gethsemani, preached a good homily and kept it sober and dignified. It all went well and it was rich in significant things for us. There was a Mozart interlude while the priests got out of their vestments for the burying and it sat well on the heart.[13]

This reminiscence borders on the irreverent, though it touches deftly enough on the absurdity that was a significant theme in so many of Father Matthew's reflections on death at the time. In a meditation on the Litany of the Saints ("From a sudden and unprovided death, deliver us, Lord"), Father Matthew recalled the strange suddenness of Merton's demise:

Father Louis's (Thomas Merton's) death was sudden. One thinks of it also as provident and provided. His whole Asian journey was a pilgrimage, so his state of soul would have been appropriate to any design of God, the point of pilgrimage, which is what Jean Leclercq had in mind, presumably, when told the news of Bangkok, "C'est magnifique! How splendid a leave taking," as if Father Louis had staged it.[14]

This comment calls to mind a trip of Father Matthew's own, years earlier, when, traveling by horseback, he stopped in at the home of a Seventh Day Adventist preacher to get out of the rain. Decrying small talk, the preacher opined, "It's gonna be a Great Day. . . . You know. Armageddon, the Valley of Jehosephat, and the Final Judgment." "I was so taken aback I laughed," Father Matthew recalls:

[13] Matthew Kelty, "A Letter on the Death of Thomas Merton," from *Sermons in a Monastery*, 77–78.

[14] Matthew Kelty, "A Great Day," in *Gethsemani Homilies*, 161.

He was puzzled that I laughed. I told him that Catholics believed in the Second Coming as much as he did and were doing it long before there were any Seventh Day Adventists. "He will come again to judge the living and the dead, and his Kingdom will have no end." It's in the Mass. "We wait in joyful hope for the coming of our Savior." "But," I said, "we hardly have it up front all the time."[15]

The Adventist was speaking of the Final End, of Armageddon and apocalyptic fire. Father Matthew was thinking of the smaller fires to which I referred at the beginning of this chapter, the fire that consumes us personally, in death. And to that degree, he came to a new appreciation of the Protestant preacher, and of Merton:

> Death is our first encounter with the Last Day. Advent is preparation for such, *both our own and the ultimate.* We are deeply involved in both. We shall all die in turn, and we will be present at the Last Great Day. However late, however early, and assuredly sudden, whenever.[16]

To be able to see death as participation in, involvement with, the Last Day is altogether remarkable. Father Matthew seems to have moved very far from the fear and trembling that he experienced alongside the train tracks in blood-soaked snow. Gethsemani, his life there, had changed him:

> It was a significant trip for Father Louis. And his last. It's gonna be a Great Day, as the man said. Sudden if it be, if it must. Provided for, certainly. Hopefully, not too soon. There's no hurry.[17]

Moving from ice to fire, Father Matthew now sees Merton's strange, and in some ways quite awful, death as providential,

[15] Kelty, "A Great Day," 162.
[16] Kelty, "A Great Day," 162, emphasis mine.
[17] Kelty, "A Great Day," 163.

caught up in the all-embracing love of everlasting mercy. From
the perspective of eternity, such petty distinctions as fast or
slow, today or tomorrow, count for little. But this requires a
God's-eye perspective, difficult to maintain for those of us earth
bound. The elements conflict; ours work at cross-purposes.

Father Matthew thought long and deeply about the Roman
Church's relation to Protestantism. How could he not, living
as a Cistercian monk in the Baptist bedrock of the central
Kentucky hills? He always knew Martin Luther to have been
a good monk, obedient to Christ if not to Papacy, and Augustinian to a fault. It was as a monk that he connected to Luther,
and it was the disassembly of the ecclesial world—of saints,
pilgrimages, and monasteries—that he most regretted about
the Reformation. Ecumenical in all things, willing even to learn
from a Seventh Day Adventist hell-bent on Armageddon,
Father Matthew saw Christianity's many-splendored wayfar-
ing as a fact with which to deal, and from which to learn.

Protestants, he notes,

> have direct access to God and that enables one to have a
> strong personal experience. But the loss of ritual, the loss of
> sacramental tradition, is dangerous under stressful condi-
> tions. Ritual is a psychic machinery by which the believer
> can get close to God, to the fire, without getting burnt. . . .
> The Protestant stands alone before God. This is the strength
> and weakness of Protestantism.[18]

Getting close to the fire. This meditation comes from an essay
appropriately entitled "Touching Fire." How can one touch
fire and not be consumed? This question was first posed when
God revealed Godself to Moses at Sinai.

Father Matthew has a quirky and really rather hilarious way
of getting into that question. There are two kinds of travelers
to the Holy Land, he observes: the tourists and the pilgrims.

---

[18] Kelty, "Touching Fire," in *Gethsemani Homilies*, 149.

"A tourist moves from the center of his existence to the periphery. He is on vacation. A pilgrim moves from the periphery, to the center of the world, his home."[19] But something happens with surprising frequency to the Holy Land pilgrim: he or she goes temporarily, stark raving mad:

> Overwhelmed by profound spiritual experience, they come suddenly to fancy themselves Jesus, Mary, the Messiah, or one of the prophets. The treatment is not difficult; it is effective. Usually it is all over in a week and becomes total and final when they leave. They return to normal and wonder whatever happened to them. People in the Israel tourist trade are familiar with all this, called popularly the "Jerusalem Syndrome," and know all the telltale signs. The first is to fall behind your tour group. Then irritation with them all. Then comes preaching. Finally, one goes around in a bed sheet. . . . People get too close to fire and catch on fire themselves.[20]

But there is a further aspect to consider here: "Ninety-five percent of the cases are Protestant," Matthew observes. This is altogether remarkable, and Father Matthew remarks well upon it. At the heart of the Protestant Reformation lay a vast reduction in ritual and ceremony. This ritual and dramatic form enabled Christians to contain the fire, to work up a sort of controlled spiritual burn, if you will.

The Holy Spirit is often represented as flame in early Christian imagery. So, what can contain the divine fire? Spirit alone. Spirit does not burn.

[19] Kelty, "Touching Fire," 148.
[20] Kelty, "Touching Fire," 148.

4. Air

The moon has gone down
and the Pleiades. Middle-night.
Hours come and go.
And I sleep alone.

Sappho of Lesbos, Fragment #168B

May the rising sun brighten all your days.
May the moon soften the darkness of your nights. Amen.

Father Matthew Kelty, "Our Last Christmas with Dom James,"
from Sermons in a Monastery, 87

❖ ❖ ❖ ❖ ❖

I return briefly now to that awe-ing moment of divine creation, when we first meet God's spirit hovering over the face of a formless abyss. There is water below, wind above. The spirit of God is called *ru'ach* in the Hebrew (*ru'ach Elohim*, Gen 1:2); then later, after God separated the waters and enabled dry land to appear, God took to the tending of this land. Even before there was a paradise-garden, God's attention turned to creation of a very special kind. Giving *form* to the clay (that same phrase, again, as if God were an artist giving form to crude matter), God breathed the spirit of life (or soul, *nephesh*) into the clay (*adamah*), and thereby the man (*adam*) was vivified (Gen 2:7). Matter plus soul equals man.

The spirit (*ru'ach*) of God, and the soul (*nephesh*) of humanity: the relationship between these two empowering and creative energies is uncertain, but potentially, at least, they may share a common creative power. The Hebrew word for spirit (*ru'ach*) also connotes wind, and hence breath. It is poetically significant that God *breathed* the soul (*nephesh*) into the man. The primary question posed by the story of creation in the book of Genesis is thus whether God and humanity can possibly inhabit the same single, creative spirit. Its answer is uncertain.

The Hellenistic Greeks were profound and prodigious translators. That marvel of ancient translation, the Greek Septuagint, has an interesting way of dealing with this story. In this Greek rendition, the Hebrew word for "spirit" (*ru'ach*) became the Greek *pneuma* (*pneuma theou*), and the Hebrew word for "soul" (*nephesh*) became the Greek *psychê*. If anything, the Greek phrasing intensified the breathlessness of the moment: "and God formed the man [*anthrôpos*] from the clay of the earth [*choun apo tês gês*] and breathed on [*enephysêsen*] his face with the breath of life [*pnoên zôês*], and the man [*anthrôpos*] became living in soul [*eis psychên zôsan*]." This would have been the biblical creation story as the early followers of Jesus knew it. Later still, in the Latin Vulgate, "spirit" was to be *spiritus*, and "soul" was to be *anima*. Father Matthew reflected endlessly on the mysteries of this personal (or trans-personal) anima and its relation to "Holy Spirit."

This mysterious notion of "spirit," *holy spirit*, weaves its way through the texts of the New Testament in ways that are very difficult to comprehend. Mark's story of Jesus begins with his baptism—"of John in Jordan," as the King James version has it—and Mark alone reports that what happened there was that the heavens opened, spirit descended, and Jesus was informed privately that he was God's son (Mark 1:9-11). The Synoptic Jesus, customarily so forgiving—even to the point of scandal— rather mysteriously claims that there is one single sin that will not be forgiven: blasphemy against holy spirit (Matt 12:31-32; Mark 3:28-30; Luke 12:10). In John's version of the salvation story, after the crucifixion and the rising, Jesus appeared to be in the process of some kind of transformation, into a being at once more spiritual and more strange; imitating the creating God of Genesis, Jesus breathes on his followers and commands them to receive holy spirit (John 20:17, 22). Peter respired in that docile spirit in the bucolic letters that bear his name (1 Pet 4:6; 2 Pet 1:21-22). So did James (Jas 4:5-6), and so did John (1 John 4; Rev 1:10). Paul rather obliquely distinguished between spirit (*pneumatikon*) bodies and soul (*psychikon*) bodies (1 Cor 15:42-44, but see 1 Thess 5:23). After the risen Christ's time with his apostles was fulfilled and he left them for the final time, the gift of holy spirit dropped on the Jerusalem community like a bombshell (Acts 2:1-42). Those not yet in on the new spiritual reality thought they were drunk, or else stark raving mad. These spirited people spoke in their varied and varying languages, and yet everyone understood what was said. This gift had something importantly to do with translation, and with the new kinds of cosmopolitan communion that this gift was to make possible.

The problem of human community—any such community, but perhaps especially the monastic sort—is the problem of politics. There may be one spirit of Christ, but there are a plurality of individual wills, or souls, and they do not always align. Hegel famously proposed that the central revelation of Greek tragedy was that it understood there to be more than one will in the world, and it places such wills in collision on stage, in order to show us all of the possible outcomes.[1] Many of them are not pretty.

Father Matthew contends that the problem of community, never easy, is exacerbated in the life of a monastic community precisely because of the anima. It is no mere coincidence that he turned to these reflections shortly after his arrival in Papua New Guinea in 1973: that is, shortly after his *departure* from

---

[1] For more in Hegel's theories about tragedy and their extension to the gospels, see Louis A. Ruprecht, Jr., *Tragic Posture and Tragic Vison: Against the Modern Failure of Nerve* (New York: Continuum, 1994), 71–127. This was to be the book I gifted to Father Matthew after our first meeting.

such a community. He stayed away for nine years, returning from his life as a solitary to the Abbey of Gethsemani in 1982, when he began to feel guilty about it all and believed it was high time to return to some form of more collective work: the work of community among his brothers. That much of that work would entail preaching and Divine Offices is something for which we may be most grateful, to him and to the community that enabled him.

In a central section of *Flute Solo* entitled "The Destroying Angel," Father Matthew utilized the psychic space provided by his newfound solitude to reflect on anima, the particular anima of the monastic personality:

> Monks by and large are artists, poets. They are heavy with anima, sons of strong mothers. They are romantics, idealists, dreamers. They must be. If they were practical men of affairs they would have gone out and done something more useful than chant psalms in the night, spend a lifetime making cheese for Christ's sake.
>
> If they are anima men, you can be sure they know the dark demon of destruction. And if they do, you can guess them generally hopeless in the give and take, the strife, contention, and controlled aggression that is essential to a good community discussion. I am sure most of them hate the whole business. They'd sooner suffer the whims of an abbot (they are all whimsical) than bear the venom of their own and another's abysmal spirit.[2]

The starting point for these reflections was also the starting point of Greek politics: democratic deliberation and debate. Father Matthew suggests that monks are generally bad at it, though the post-Vatican II reforms had endeavored to make monastic life more democratic and left less to the whims and

---

[2] Matthew Kelty, "Flute Solo," in *My Song is of Mercy*, 56–57; see also 71: "I suppose a priest, like a monk, like a prophet, a poet, a dreamer, a solitary, is a jarring note, a disturbing nonconformist voice. Possibly he frightens people. I have been frightened myself."

vagaries of their abbots. The discussion in the chapter house, among monks otherwise committed to a life of studied silence, could be difficult. Not everyone wanted democracy; not everyone was prepared for the time and energy it took. Better the easy autocracy of an avowed and silent obedience.

That is certainly part of what Father Matthew is saying here, and it may help to explain why he was so much more favorably disposed to his previous abbot, Dom James, than Thomas Merton had been.[3] Father Matthew felt that his former abbot inhabited his authority with the right balance and in the right way. But this is a relatively easy thing to say when the abbot is no longer abbot and you are living as a solitary halfway around the world. There must be more to it than this.

Father Matthew appreciated the work of Carl Jung and found great psychological insight in his religious reflections on archetypes. Here Father Matthew seems to be grappling with an archetypal personality type, one embodied in poets, visual artists, scholars, monks. They tend to be bad organizers, too solitary for collective work. They tend to be too self-absorbed in their own monumental tasks and their often elevated sense of ego and entitlement. And they, all of them, are thus uniquely susceptible to what he here calls "the destroying angel":

> The destroying angel that accompanies every person of the spirit is a real danger. Mere intellectual grasp of the concept will not do. Neither can will power avail. It is a matter mostly of prayer, a wrestling with demons, with Christ and his grace.
>
> Not a few monks leave the monastery because of the destroying angel. He drives them out; I am quite certain of that. Not all of them, to be sure, for some should leave. But when

[3] See, for instance, "Our Last Christmas with Dom James," in *Sermons in a Monastery*, 82–87, from which I quoted at the outset of this chapter, as well as "Come and See" and "Change" in that same volume (25–31), plus "On Dom James," in *My Song is of Mercy*, 122–24.

a person approaches God, the enemy has a way of capital-
izing on the utter unworthiness of the lover to the point that
the lover cannot abide it. One needs a sort of compassion
for poets and priests and artists. We do not realize what a
precious gift they are to humanity. Or what a burden they
bear.[4]

The point, like the prose, is subtle. Father Matthew is a monk;
monks are a difficult breed, susceptible to flights of fanciful
self-importance. They are also uniquely susceptible, he has
informed us, to the destroying angel. This angel often tempts
them to leave monastic life. Father Matthew has left. So, what
is going on here?

He continues, by way of explanation:

> When I began to experience the call to solitude, and to soli-
> tude away from the monastery, I was wary of the destroying
> angel and feared that he might be deluding me. It was for
> that very reason I insisted I would never leave without the
> abbot's blessing. When my abbot did refuse his blessing, it
> hurt me, but I had no great difficulty in accepting it. This
> was not virtue, but common sense. Monks get carried away
> with all kinds of ideas. Several years later a new abbot did
> give me his blessing. This confirmed me more strongly in
> my faith in obedience as the foundation of monastic disci-
> pline. It is this sort of death in the will of God that at once
> unites the monk with Christ before the Father and puts to
> flight the evil one. Yet, it is not always easy. They did not
> name the place Gethsemani for nothing.[5]

Gethsemane: the site of Jesus's temptation, betrayal, and apparent rout. It is the most astonishing story in the gospels, one
so radical in its implications that John refused it a place in his
gospel at all. John's Jesus actually mocks the Gethsemane

---

[4] Kelty, "Flute Solo," 57–58.
[5] Kelty, "Flute Solo," 58.

prayer ("what shall I pray, take this cup away?" Jesus asks contemptuously; "No, this is why I have come").

At a minimum, we may say this. Using Hegel's ideas about tragedy, Gethsemane is the gospel's tragic epicenter, the crux in which Jesus's will and the Father's will are not in perfect alignment. Soul and spirit conflict. Jesus does not will this to happen; he begs for a way out. God's silence, together with Judas's kiss, implies a negative answer to the request. The Synoptic evangelists differ as to what this means. For Mark, Gethsemane is an occasion to highlight the absolutely shattering experience of betrayal, loss, isolation, and crucifixion ("My God, my God, why have you abandoned me?" Mark 15:34). For Matthew, whose divided Jesus is weak in flesh but strong in spirit, it is an opportunity to show how the Hebrew Scriptures have been ironically fulfilled through such a scandal ("how then should the scriptures be fulfilled, that it must be so?" Matt 26:54). For Luke, Gethsemane displays the power of prayer, through which Jesus acquires the anticipatory resoluteness to face his fate after all ("into your hands I commit my spirit," Luke 23:46).[6]

Father Matthew's phrasing brilliantly captures this paradox: "It is this sort of death in the will of God that at once unites the monk with Christ before the Father and puts to flight the evil one." "Death in the will of God" is an oblique way to suggest how the realignment of soul and spirit may operate. As many artists have noted, the self must exit so that spirit may enter.[7] Failing that, there are simply too many voices in our head.

---

[6] Ruprecht, *Tragic Posture and Tragic Vision*, 181–229.

[7] I am thinking particularly of Maya Deren, whose reflections on the power of Vodou ritual dance and possession-performance were exceptionally forward-looking. See Maya Deren, *Divine Horsemen: The Living Gods of Haiti* (Kingston, NY: Documentext, 1953), 247–62, as well as *The Essential Maya Deren* (Kingston, NY: Documentext, 2005), 127–28, 185.

The Abbey of Gethsemani is named by, and claimed by, this pivotal story. Father Matthew describes his decision to leave it for a time as a Gethsemane-moment, a moment of maximal solitude and self-doubt. And then later, of sudden spiritual realignment.

There is a moving sculpture in the hills near the abbey that depicts the failed disciples sleeping in Gethsemane in the very moment when their Lord has told them most emphatically to "watch." Father Matthew meditated long on this image:

> The disciples did not fall asleep at Gethsemani or at Tabor because they were tired. No. They were simply overcome, overwhelmed, and could not cope. So they turned off and went to sleep.[8]

The New Testament writers sometimes refer to death as a falling asleep. Death is often depicted in Greek terms as breath leaving the body once and for all, and the bodily clay returning to the ground from which it came. The Genesis cycle is circular. God's spirit hovered above over the waters below. God formed land, formed man, breathed life. Sin, and mortality, came next. The destroying angel.

The breath is ephemeral; the spirit is not.

[8] Matthew Kelty, "Believing in Love," in *Gethsemani Homilies*, 57.

Interlude
Matthew and Merton

One of the most striking things about Christianity, at least as it presents itself in the New Testament, is that the movement had not one founding figure, but two: Jesus, and Paul.

They are profoundly different characters, in very many ways. Jesus is unanimously depicted as scandalously irreverent and virtually dismissive of the details of Jewish law; Paul was thoroughly trained in a most rigorous school of that law. Jesus is depicted in the Synoptic gospels, especially Luke's, as surrounded always (scandalously, again) by women who appear to be free to travel with him and who follow him even to Jerusalem, and the cross. Paul possesses a far more complicated, and regulated, view of gender relations, notoriously insisting in one place that women remain separate and silent in churches. Jesus demonstrates no great interest in sexual regulations, going so far as to forgive a woman's adulterous liaison, as reported in John's gospel; Paul, by contrast, seems singularly preoccupied with sex, notoriously insisting in one place that marriage is simply a way to legitimate sexual contact between couples too weak to remain celibate. Whereas they both speak with command and authority, Jesus is depicted in the Synoptic gospels as a forceful speaker whose most memorable parables and homespun insights are short on density but long on human insight; Paul, by contrast, was trained in Stoic philosophy, and it shows. He often adopts a philosophical vocabulary as his own, especially when making densely philosophical arguments about the relations between Jews and Gentiles, or about salvation history in God's time.

Father Matthew collided with another towering anima, one that constituted an essential aspect of his Gethsemani. I am speaking, of course, of Thomas Merton. I would like to use the contrast between Jesus and Paul as one way with which to make sense of the complex relationship between these two towering figures from the Abbey of Gethsemani: Father Louis (Thomas Merton, 1915–1968) and Father Matthew (Charles Kelty, 1915–2011). In the terms I have set out above, particularly that last one, Merton seems a deeply Pauline figure, a philosopher deeply interested in thinking multiple religious traditions (mainly Buddhism and Roman Catholicism) in tandem. Father Matthew, by contrast, was, and remained, a Jesus man. Father Matthew's writings possess the same parabolic insight and quiet humor that Jesus's Synoptic speaking possesses. Merton's writings are more elliptical, more challenging, and more philosophically grounded. And yet—this will be something we will need to come back to—both men were ultimately poets.

The Roman Church has an interesting way of dealing with this dualistic ecclesial reality. Utilizing the apostle Peter as a sort of stand-in for the earthly Jesus, Rome places Peter and Paul at the very foundation of the city, the Church, and thus the Christian world. Peter, the brash and headstrong disciple who was especially loved even in the midst of his shortcomings and who, according to Matthew's gospel, was nicknamed "Rock" in order to become the bedrock on which Jesus intended to establish his church. Paul, by contrast, who never met the earthly Jesus, and who began his career by targeting Peter and his friends as heterodox threats to orthodox Judaism and the law, managed in the end to claim an apostolic authority equal to Peter's—no mean feat. And in so doing, he actually convinced Peter as to the merits of his "gospel," with its inclusion of Greeks in the new way of God's relating to the world made available by Jesus. (Peter, we should recall, might have trumped every argument by simply saying that he'd asked Jesus about this very thing, and the Lord had said what Peter says—to his credit, he never played that card.)

The two men are depicted in dramatically different ways in Rome. Peter is benign, with soft features and a gently furrowed brow emanating care and concern; he holds the keys to the church vouchsafed him by his Lord. Paul, by contrast, is severe, powerful, threatening; he holds a sword, a large one, allegedly to commemorate his own beheading in this same city. Peter, by contrast, is said to have been crucified upside down. Both died, and were buried, in Rome; the two largest churches in the city were erected over their tombs—one (Peter's) inside the city's Aurelian walls, the other (Paul's) outside.

It is hard not to hear, in Father Matthew's eloquent reflections on Peter and Paul, a veiled understanding of his own evolving relationship with Merton, and what they both meant to the evolving community at Gethsemani:

> Peter as man among others is surely a #4 on the Enneagram: ardent, impulsive, terrified of tough women, enthusiastic, responsive, gullible and naive. It is not difficult to understand his admiration for Paul: the idealist, the Puritan prophet and preacher, staunch defender of the truth, the zealot. A real Enneagram #1. Paul: vigorous, tireless, passionate and consumed in his commitment to truth as he saw it. Worn out in the service of the Gospel, and frequently reminding us of it, fearless before Peter, righteous, forthright.
>
> And yet, they loved one another, needed one another.
>
> Paul had his world turned around in a moment. Peter gave his world away without 10 seconds hesitation, the fisherman's world he knew just as quickly as the apostle's world he entered on. The same Peter who wore grooves in his cheeks in a life's tears of regret. Paul needed Peter's warmth; Peter needed Paul's courage.
>
> Totally different, totally Christ's in the end.[1]

---

[1] Matthew Kelty, "Sts. Peter and Paul," in *My Song is of Mercy*, 144.

Or, consider this:

> Hence, to look on Peter and Paul in some honesty is to tune in to the play of God in human history. Peter was an unlikely prospect for any serious endeavor: charming, generous, enthusiastic, but steady, fickle, and cowardly. To him were entrusted the keys. Paul was a proud bigot, self-righteous, vindictive, and prone to posturing. Yet he was chosen to be the apostle to the Gentiles. With such material the power of God made heroes. They were the very human foundation of a very human Church which is at once the presence and power of Christ on earth.
>
> If all you see is present reality, you do not see at all. If you are blind to the mystical dimension of the human scene, you might as well be physically blind for all the good it does you. We need and are nourished by the depths of faith. This feast of Peter and Paul is a call to that.[2]

Matthew's ultimate point here is plain: "The mystery of Peter and Paul is no greater than our own."[3] The "us" in this instance may well be intended for Matthew and Merton.

But how, if indeed Peter and Paul came to love one another, how did this love come about? The New Testament does not tell us. We see them argue, and we see this argument exclusively from Paul's perspective. He writes about it, and so does his sponsor, Luke. We do not hear Peter's side of the matter. Similarly, we may be put to wonder, if Matthew and Merton came to love one another, then how did that come about? Merton did not write much about Matthew,[4] but Matthew, who

---

[2] Matthew Kelty, "Indifferent Sickness," in *Gethsemani Homilies*, 43–44.

[3] Kelty, "Indifferent Sickness," 43.

[4] In Merton's journal from his final year, much preoccupied in December and January with the election of a new abbot and the end of Dom James's tenure, under which he bristled, Merton sought out Matthew's counsel and impressions: "Father Matthew has some good ideas, but is too volatile. He hasn't a chance" (Thomas Merton, *The Other Side of the Mountain*, ed. Patrick Hart [New York: HarperCollins Publishers, 1998], 25). Clearly, Matthew had more "piss and vinegar" in his veins in his early years at Gethsemani, as Merton would have understood well.

survived him by more than forty years, had occasion to reflect many times on Merton.

Two more divergent characters are scarcely imaginable: Merton, the orphaned child of two bohemian artists; Matthew, the child of a relatively stable but clandestinely immodest couple.[5] Merton, the charismatic carouser and womanizer. Matthew, the gay recluse (I will have a good deal more to say about this in Chapter Six). Merton, the dramatic convert to the Roman faith, whose nearly Augustinian catalogue of his own halting way toward conversion, *The Seven Storey Mountain*, made him famous for all the wrong reasons. Matthew, quietly born and bred in the Irish Church in Boston. Merton the mountain-man, and Matthew, born of the sea. Matthew considered Merton too brooding, too self-important and precious at times, too intellectual, too English; he saw himself as an intuitive Celt, an elemental creature of the Irish soil. He said all of this many times.[6]

The two men met when Matthew joined the Abbey of Gethsemani and Merton was assigned as his novice master. Matthew seemed to recall the experience as torture, nothing less:

> The lasting memory I had of him concerned an incident during Lent. During Lent there is fasting and you get hungry and a little tired and irritable and impatient. On a dreadful day when its [*sic*] about twenty-five degrees outside, and a wind blowing in from Canada, he sends you out with a bush hook which is so dull you can't cut anything with it, to cut bushes from the hillside. Really make-do work, cleaning up the hillside. And then the next day with the bright sunshine and crocus beginning to show and spring is coming, and its

[5] See the shattering tale told in Matthew Kelty, "Abortion: A Personal Experience," in *Gethsemani Homilies*, 120–21.

[6] See, for example, Matthew Kelty, *Gethsemani Homilies*, xvii–xviii; *Sermons in a Monastery: Chapter Talks*, ed. William O. Paulsell, Cistercian Studies 58 (Kalamazoo, MI: Cistercian Publications, 1983), 77–79; and *My Song is of Mercy*, 11–14, 93–95, 111–12.

[sic] fifty degrees outside, just beginning to get warm, and he sends me upstairs to type. I can't type. I hunt and peck and he wants me to type his manuscripts on A.B. Dick stencils. He was never satisfied with what he wrote. He would redo it; he would make a few corrections on this page, but major corrections on the back of the previous page. So you are typing along on this page and then you realize, you forgot the insert. He never shortened; he always expanded and added whole paragraphs in writing I couldn't read. . . . He was terrible to work for. I used to dread that.[7]

This not-so-subtle harassment reaches a kind of peak during the Lenten fast. Merton informs Matthew that he will type. Matthew refuses. Merton says it a second time. Again, Matthew refuses. A third time; Matthew relents:

No one else would have tolerated that, if you had said "No." It was an order. Three times. I think that was it if I had done it again. The end! I never forgot that. Other monks still remember that exchange.

But Merton could understand a forty-five-year-old man who was new and hungry and tired and irritable or whatever and was asked to do something that he found very difficult. He was tolerant enough to appreciate that and to give me a break. Most people wouldn't have bothered. I wouldn't.[8]

This is all subtly crafted and orchestrated. Refusal three times. "Before the cock crows twice you will deny me thrice" in the Authorized Version's fine phasing. Matthew has placed himself in the role I have already suggested for him: Peter, as yet unschooled and nearly undone. (And if this is right, then Merton has been made a Christ-figure of sorts in this singular story.)

---

[7] Matthew Kelty, "Introduction," in *Gethsemani Homilies*, xvii–xviii.
[8] Kelty, "Introduction," xviii.

I suspect another subtle clue as to how this relationship deepened and how the two men came to love one another may be found in Matthew's meditations on, of all things, baby bears:

> A bear will cuff a cub to teach it manners. To curb its asser-tion. To teach it to live with others and save strength. A good mother will cuff a daughter, a father a son, to teach breeding. Not violence, that is savage. But love, by teaching the neces-sity of restraint. To heed others. To live in communion. The more so with the gifted whom we all admire and none admonish. Otherwise the child becomes an adult who must always have his way. Cannot dialogue. Cannot abide criti-cism. Pouts and is full of self-pity when crossed. A terrible handicap. . . .
>
> Peter was such. Gifted. Given to impulse. Generous. As-sertive. And with no sense. Jesus knew his man, though, knew he was a prince. But too full of ego, too impetuous to be sure. . . .
>
> So Peter learned, if late. Jesus was no put-down artist, but Peter was the uncuffed cub, full of self and self-assertion, ready to wilt at someone critical.
>
> Angels come to us sometimes. Sometimes in a startling way. . . .
>
> [And so] we can learn. We can grow. If as cubs we were not cuffed, the cuffing comes later if we accept it. Peter did. And died Rock of the Church. Martyred for Christ. This is the month of the angels. They'll be around.[9]

Matthew was the uncuffed cub when he joined the Abbey of Gethsemani in February of 1960. Merton cuffed him, clearly more than once. Matthew bristled, but he bore it; he listened, and he learned. In this sense, then, Merton was Matthew's angel, his guardian and his stalwart hope. There are surely lesser legacies to honor.

---

[9] Matthew Kelty, "Of Angels and Bears," in *My Song is of Mercy*, 196–201.

This is evident in the way Matthew recalled Merton in later years. He grew to appreciate the man's aptitude for snap judgment and immediate, unsolicited action. Merton could put down in the right moment and he could lift up. But the greatest gift that Matthew's long fellowship with Merton provided was, paradoxically enough, the gift of solitude:

> Yet the greatest gift I had not asked for, had not expected. That gift was an understanding of the role of solitude in monastic life, in a person's life. It was Thomas Merton who taught me this, both in the days I was a novice under his direction, as also in later years in a study of his writings. Probably the most significant work of this man lay in his return to the solitary aspect of monasticism. The results of this awakening, this rediscovery, have only begun to be manifest. I am sure it is only a beginning.
>
> It is necessary to see how original he was in this. By reason of his own charisma and his study of early sources of monastic life, be brought back to life this element that had practically disappeared. It was neither easy nor pleasant, for many opposed him.
>
> Thomas Merton was arguing not merely for a revival of the eremitic life within the order, but also for a return to the spirit of solitude that from the earliest times had been characteristic of monastic life, of Cistercian life. His writings and studies of this were many and good.
>
> Now, some years after his death and the spreading of his teaching, it is somewhat difficult to recapture the situation on which he dwelt, for Gethsemani has since undergone both an external and internal renovation that is phenomenal. But at that time monastic life there, as at most monasteries of the kind for the past several centuries, had been warped in favor of community. Monks literally did everything in common. . . .
>
> Merton put his finger on a weak spot. He knew that as long as that weakness was not corrected, all was not well. Monastic life is not just a group of ascetics, people accustomed to hard labor, indifferent to scant food, great stretches

of formal prayer and liturgical ceremony, multiple obser-
vances and customs in a controlled environment. To some
extent it is all that, but that is not the whole of it. . . .

He did not think that living in a silent community was
necessarily an adequate expression of solitude, though this
had long been maintained. He thought the person in monastic life needed real solitude; that is, time alone. And further, and even more important, he needed to be schooled in
what to do with that exposure. The greatest lesson Thomas
Merton taught me was the fruitful use of solitude.[10]

Thomas Merton was the crux of a radical (re)formation of
the monastery, and that reformed monastery was to be the crux
of Matthew's own subsequent formation. Through this shift
to solitude, Matthew too would devote long years to the eremitic life, primarily as a solitary in Papua New Guinea from
1973 to 1982 (he eventually had his own small hermitages at
Gethsemani as well, as we have seen). And he would eventually discover himself to be an artist, a talker, and a writer, much
as Merton had been. No Merton, no Matthew; it's that simple.

This was the realization that Matthew experienced during
Holy Week in 1973, freshly arrived in Papua New Guinea just
five years after Merton's sudden death. Later years would
bring further insight. Thirty years later, in 1998, he would come
to a deeper appreciation of Merton's spiritual discernment:

Instant grasp of the situation.
Instant response.
Total indifference to the consequences. . . .
I dare say Merton lived [this] way. As delicate as a wind
chime to any breath of the Spirit.[11]

He also grew to appreciate the discipline that had once
seemed churlish and overly intellectual to him; a survey of

[10] Matthew Kelty, "Flute Solo," in *My Song is of Mercy*, 12–14.
[11] Matthew Kelty, "Love in Depth," in *Gethsemani Homilies*, 115.

Merton's prodigious correspondence taught Matthew that.[12] He learned to love some of the writers Merton loved too, like Camus.[13] Yet the crux of the thing was apparent to Matthew almost immediately, in the dreadful days following Merton's death:

> I do not know how to summarize the man; the thought is not even decent. Except to say that he was a contradiction. He lived at the center of the cross where the two arms meet. Maybe, you could say, at the heart of life. My guess is that at no other place is contradiction reconciled.
>
> He was a problem to many here and elsewhere. I know the reason for the problem: I mean the terrifying tensions the man endured with a kind of courage only the power of God made possible. I kept feeling when close to him that God is near. And to be near God is to be near something at once wonderful and terrible. Like fire. It burns. . . .
>
> The only way I could live with the man was to love him whole, as he was, with all his contradictions, and I think this is the only way to understand him. That is the way he loved me.
>
> He was as merry a man as I have known, yet he had depths of sadness it were best not to mention. He loved the monastic life, yet lived in it in a style all his own. He had a real love for the solitary life, and yet no one around here has his kind of love for people, for the world God made. . . .
>
> I cannot go on. You do not get this kind of person from the hands of God very often. He is a living witness for God, for Gethsemani, for the monastic life, for the church, for the world. Praised be God in his saints forever and ever. Amen.[14]

[12] Matthew Kelty, "The Hidden Ground of Love," in *My Song is of Mercy*, 93–95.

[13] Matthew Kelty, "The Plague" and "The Dinner Party," in *Sermons in a Monastery*, 48–55, 91–98.

[14] Matthew Kelty, "A Letter on the Death of Thomas Merton," in *Sermons in a Monastery*, 78–79.

It is difficult to know what tensions and sadness Matthew had in mind, though it bears keeping in mind that Matthew had been serving as Merton's confessor for the previous six months, so he knew whereof he spoke. While Matthew made little of it, Merton's selection of him for this role speaks volumes. "Merton asked me to be his confessor," Matthew recalled years later, "not because he needed me but because he knew I needed him."[15]

The two men clearly developed a deep rapport, one bound by their silence and their solitude as much as anything. It was an elemental connection, both subliminal and sublime. They liked the same poetry and the same kinds of jazz, and Merton owned both a record player and loads of books. While Matthew may not seem to have been as taken with Merton's interfaith explorations ("People buy into it, pay for it, eat it up. So Augustine did and got so tangled he was years breaking free"[16]), his own later years bespeak an increasing and more radical openness to everything from primitives and Celts, to Zen Buddhism, to Taoism and the rest.

How did Peter and Paul come to love one another? *Elementally*. Mutually. Not with communication only, but with communion. By having a sacred task in common:

"The only way I could live with the man was to love him whole, as he was, with all his contradictions, and I think this is the only way to understand him. That is the way he loved me." So said, and so loved, both men.

---

[15] As quoted by Judith Hardcastle in *We Are Already One: Thomas Merton's Message of Hope*, ed. Gray Henry and Jonathan Montaldo (Louisville, KY: Fons Vitae: Center for Interfaith Relations, 2014), 122.

[16] Matthew Kelty, "Taking up the Cross," in *Gethsemani Homilies*, 108.

PART TWO

The Spiritual

5. Art

I stand among you as one who offers a small message of hope that, first, there are always people who dare to seek on the margins of society, who are not dependent on social acceptance, nor dependent on social routine, and prefer a kind of free-floating existence under a state of risk. And among these people, if they are faithful to their own calling, to their own vocation and to their own message from God, communication on the deepest level is possible.

And the deepest level of communication is not communication, but communion. It is wordless. It is beyond words, and it is beyond speech, and it is beyond concept. Not that we discover a new unity. We discover an older unity. My dear brothers and sisters, we are already one. But we imagine that we are not. So what we have to recover is our original unity. What we have to be is what we are.

Thomas Merton, *The Asian Journal*, 307–8

❖ ❖ ❖ ❖ ❖

Consider Leonardo Da Vinci tweaking the Mona Lisa's half-smile. Consider Michelangelo retouching the point of near-contact between God's and Adam's hands on the Sistine ceiling. Consider Caravaggio executing the wound in Christ's side into which Thomas is inserting his doubting finger. In each case, the same question: *how did they know they were finished*? What last brushstroke convinced them that to do any more would change the thing, but without improving the thing? When is a work of art complete?

The same question can be put to other fine arts. When has a poet's painstaking search for the right word and the right rhythm come to an end? When is a poem finished? When is a sonnet complete? Or a sonata? A concerto? An opera? There is something as arbitrary as it is mysterious at work here, in the question of how such judgments are made. As the Romantic philosophers knew well, art and religion and philosophy are all spiritual (*geistige*) pursuits, each of them uniquely creative and singularly human. There is both pride and wonderment in that fact.

Father Matthew knew this well. "Art is nothing if not an expression of the spirit: that is what produced it in the first place."[1] He toyed often, as we have already seen, with the typology of the artistic and monastic personality, the anima they have in common. The monk as artist. The monastic life as purposeless purpose. The contemplative life as silent poetry. Every monk's solitude producing *monaulia*, "flute music." This is a potent constellation of interests and ideas.

And it all begins with the decision to enter a monastery in the first place, to take up the rigors of monastic life. We may put the same question we put to Leonardo, Michelangelo, and Caravaggio. When does the monk know that it is time to go? For a great deal goes into this decision, and, while it may not

---

[1] Matthew Kelty, "Dreams and Visions and Voices," in *My Song is of Mercy*, 88. His reasoning is striking and far-reaching: "Nor will merely keeping up old traditions matter much if the heart is gone out of them. They may become commercially useful and draw tourists, but in terms of real culture this is a travesty, almost a sacrilege. The culture is not kept alive by such tactics. Even art will die. The old patterns may be repeated and the old forms reproduced, but if the spirit dies, the art dies with it. Art is nothing if not an expression of the spirit; that is what produced it in the first place." In other words, no spirit, no novelty, just dead form. The religious life is an art form. Spiritual truth is new or not at all.

be irreversible, it comes close to being so. The Sistine Chapel now belongs to the pope . . . and to the ages. The monk's life and livelihood, his anima, now belongs to the divine. This is strong medicine, hard to swallow even for those most in need of the curative of solitude, silence, obedience. The monastic life is hard, entire.

When I spent some time in exploration at Mount Athos, that great monastic center of the Eastern Orthodox world, I met an American monk who had received the name of Father Moses. I had just arrived at the Iviron Monastery and wished to take a walk outside the walls before they closed at sunset. As I was leaving the precinct, a monk was entering: non-descript, with the same salt-and-pepper hair in a bun, the same wire-rimmed spectacles, and the same long dark robes as all the others. He was a monk, generically so, to my eye. Then I heard a question put, after we passed one another, in perfect American English, "Where in the world are you from?" We talked until nearly dawn the next day.

He was born and raised in San Francisco, and much of his adult life had been constituted by a series of irreversible decisions. He decided to convert to Orthodoxy. Shortly thereafter, he decided to become a monk. If he were to be a monk, then where better than the center of the Orthodox world: Mount Athos. When I met him, he was on leave from his monastery, wandering across the Chalkidikean peninsula in search of a hermitage. Each monastery on Athos supports a small network of caves in which the solitaries live. They produce some commodity that the monastery may sell, and the monastery provides them with food and water. They may choose to be present when the exchange of food and produce is made if they wish to engage in conversation, or they may elect to stay away in isolation. Such hermitages are fairly limited in number near these understaffed monastic communities. Father Moses was wandering until his happenstance arrival at a monastery would coincide with the death of a hermit and the concomitant freeing up of a cave cell. Like the aptly named hermit crab, he would promptly occupy the vacant cell . . . and spend the rest of his natural days there, until he died in his turn.

This is all very serious business. We spent the night talking about everything: life in the United States, life on Mount Athos, the concept of tragedy (about which I was then writing a dissertation), the philosophies of Friedrich Nietzsche and Nikos Kazantzakis, everything, so it seemed. Four days later, when I was in Daphne, the administrative center where I was to reclaim my passport as I departed the Holy Mountain, I ran into Father Moses again. He had something for me, he said, which turned out to be a prayer chord woven of black wool in the shape of a cross. He gave it to me and said, "You must never forget, when you re-enter the world, that demons and evil are real." And he was gone. The year was 1987; Merton had been dead for nearly twenty years, and Father Matthew was five years back from his second sojourn in Papua New Guinea.

Thomas Merton found the path that led him from secular world-weariness to monastic seclusion excruciating; writing about that excrucation (in *The Seven Storey Mountain*) is what made him famous. Father Matthew's path seems altogether easy and breezy, by contrast. I do not know that this is true, but so it can seem in Father Matthew's late prose. There, he clearly relishes being a monk. But his writing also strikes a more tormented note. Nearly twenty years separate his profession of vows and his arrival at the Abbey of Gethsemani. He was fourteen years a priest by then. So this was not a decision to which he instantly gravitated, as Father Moses did. Even Merton found his way to the monastery far more quickly and cleanly.

Father Matthew found the transition to monastic life difficult, to say the least, and one may well wonder whether Merton was an unusually strict taskmaster, or whether his novice was simply having trouble adapting to the life of obedience. You must give up everything. To fail to understand this is to fail to understand monastic life. It is also to fail to understand Father

Matthew. Father Matthew had not been at Gethsemani long before he first toyed with the idea of leaving. Merton resisted him.[2] So, as he has told us, did his abbot. But just five years after Merton's death, Father Matthew did leave and lived as a solitary for nine years. When he returned, things were different. No doubt the monastery was different, but so was he. He was sixty-seven years old, for a start. And he positively reveled in the monastic life for the next thirty years. The work he had to do, he did, and this freed him for the *creative* work of monastic life, his true calling. Monks, he now saw, were artists—poets, painters, what have you.[3] The Abbey of Gethsemani was, by then, an especially enriching community of artist-monks. This too formed the man we meet in these pages.

In the end, Father Matthew understood the monk to be fundamentally an artist of solitude, a practitioner of wonderment and close attention. The monastic currency is love, and the raw material is beauty, nothing less:

> Nor have we touched on beauty. What grace can compare with a speed skater on ice, a ski jumper flying through space? Think of ballet, of song and dance, or orchestra and symphony. Of the glories of art: in photography, in painting, in sculpture. All in some sense defy the laws of reality and move beyond their imposed limits.
>
> All to the glory of God.[4]

So much for love and beauty. But there is also truth, dramatic truth. And this delivers us to the crux of the mystery lying at the heart of monastic life.

---

[2] Matthew Kelty, "Flute Solo," in *My Song is of Mercy*, 11–14. See also some further relevant reflections in "A Memory of Thomas Merton," in *Gethsemani Homilies*, 169–71, and "The Dinner Party," and "The Dalai Lama and Dom Vital," from *Sermons in a Monastery*, 94–95 and 102–4.

[3] Matthew Kelty, "The Sacred Brought to Speech," in *My Song is of Mercy*, 212–14.

[4] Matthew Kelty, "Christmas Midnight Mass," in *My Song is of Mercy*, 253.

What do these monks *do* all day, apart from tending the grounds, making cheese and chocolate? Primarily, their work is one of choreography: to sing the psalms, and to celebrate the Mass, to preside at the table in the eucharistic sacrifice. It is actually astonishing how much music these monks make, and how long they have been making it. Father Matthew genuinely loved this artful aspect of the life:

> And we expedite the coming [of the Kingdom]. Are involved in it. How?
>
> Obviously, by music. By chant. By song.
>
> I call your attention to it. If it borders on the absurd to make cheese and fruitcake and fudge for the Kingdom, and we do, I call your attention to worse than that:
>
> We sing for it.
>
> This is a house of music, of song. Seven times a day we gather to sing songs.
>
> To God. To Christ. For us and for the world.
>
> I beg you, enter into the poetry of this beautiful truth.
>
> We sing for the coming of the Kingdom. It is perhaps the most significant contribution we could make.
>
> What else surpasses it in beauty and meaning?
>
> Seven times a day we gather to sing to God for the world. How practical! How down to earth! We have been doing it since we got here on December 21, 1848. The song began the next day, December 22, and has never ceased.[5]

The constancy of song and of lyric is remarkable here; equally astonishing is to realize how constantly these monks are at the table. The monks of Gethsemani celebrate the Eucharist daily, often several times; it is quite simply the sacred heart of their collective enterprise. And it involves another kind of complex antiphonic artistry. To Father Matthew's practiced eye, the great artwork that they collectively produce is a drama, a drama enacted in God's sacred tense: eternity:

---

[5] Matthew Kelty, "We Sing for the Kingdom," in *We Sing for the Kingdom*, 12–13.

There is no drama in all the world, in all time, more profound, more living, more real, than the drama enacted here
at this altar. There is nothing on earth that can come even
remotely near it. The sanctuary is the stage, the roles are
assigned. The celebrant dons a vestment, a costume. He
enacts a rite. He personifies Christ, speaks his lines, his
words. And pretends that Christ does again what he did
before. Only this drama is not just pretending. It does what
it acts. For as there is stage time that transcends time, so
there is a God time: Spirit time, grace time, eternal time. And
we enter it.

Good drama is first of all good performance. Good drama
is also participation. If the audience is not involved, there is
no drama. Good drama is life made articulate, human experience witnessed, my humanity revealed. The better the
drama, the better my entrance into it.

Good drama is first of all a quality performance. But far
more than good performance, it must also be quality participation. Here history is not reenacted, it is accomplished.
History is made. In the one action, Christ and all his mysteries. How? With us![6]

Philosophers since Plato have wondered about the relationship between a representation and the thing it represents, that
is to say, between the image and the original. Christian philosophers would enhance that speculation in order to distinguish

---

[6] Matthew Kelty, "Christmas Eve [1991]," in *My Song is of Mercy*, 219–20.
And he continues (220–21): "So we are there. If good drama be quality performance and quality participation, we are shepherds, we are wise men,
innkeeper and Bethlehemite. We hear the angels, follow the shepherds, see
the star, feel the warmth of the cattle. Not in imagination. Really. For I am
involved in this drama. He came for me. He came for you. There is no one
he did not come for.

This is not a play you just come and watch. You cannot just come and
watch. Even your watching is your languid response, your way of being
involved. You are witness, after all. You were there. You can be summoned
as witness. . . .

Drama which is history. A story which is ours. Forever. There is every
reason, then, to say as I say to you now, 'Merry Christmas.' "

between an icon and an idol, thereby demonstrating that an icon could be venerated without in any way deflating the worship of God. Romantic philosophers wondered how the kinds of image-making we meet in the visual arts, in philosophy, and in religion could be related. For Father Matthew—heir to all of this philosophical enquiry whether he admitted it or not—all three of these pursuits, as pursuits of spirit, were best conceived as *creative* arts. In performing them, human beings participate in the divine act of creation itself. All the world is peopled with artists; to be religious or philosophical is to fashion one's life as a work of art.[7]

The mysterious priestess Diotima of Mantineia plays lyrically upon this idea in Plato's densely evocative and erotic dialogue, the *Symposium*.[8] All human beings are pregnant, she suggests, desiring to create as a spiritual response to the fact of their mortality. The immortal soul wishes to leave something material behind. Physically, she observes, men and women create children; women bear this bodily burden and deliver new lives in this way. But spiritually, souls in communion create virtue; Diotima speaks of men in this context, but there is no reason to see men as the exclusive bearers of such spiritual virtue.

The question of men, and women, and of their relation to one another, has been an especially vexed one in the history of the Christian church. The religious stakes are high precisely because the creation of children and of virtue is at stake. The discussion of gender bleeds seamlessly into questions of sex and sexuality, identity and incarnation. And in these areas of

---

[7] See Alexander Nehamas, *The Art of Living: Socratic Reflections from Plato to Foucault* (Berkeley, CA: University of California Press, 1998), for the idea that there has been a sort of philosophical underground that finds its roots in Socratic reflection and embraces the art of being human as a significant task for thinking. Nehamas counts Plato, Montaigne, Nietzsche, and Foucault among them. I think of monks like Merton and Matthew as possessing this same philosophical pedigree.

[8] Plato, *Symposium* 206c–207a.

subtle interrogation, as we will see, Father Matthew was heir to the confusion of his times, and yet capable of crystalline insights of sometimes surprising moral clarity.

6. Woman

. . . the earth our mother, God our father, heaven and
earth united in prayer, the feminine and masculine one.

Matthew Kelty, "Gratefulness," in *My Song is of Mercy*, 180

❖ ❖ ❖ ❖ ❖

In thinking about men and women—their respective identi-
ties, virtues, spiritual gifts, and spiritual challenges—Father
Matthew relied on his concept of anima. His starting point was
the assumption that men and women, much like heaven and
earth, share in one another's distinctive gifts. Women have a
masculine side and men have a feminine side, he believed, and
some kind of soulful integration, while the essential spiritual
task before all of us, is seldom easy. There are many reasons
for this. The main one is decidedly cultural, a matter of patriarchy and its long after-effects:

> Relating to our other side. Coming to terms with the other
> pole of our bipolarity. In a man, this is often pictured as a
> feminine spirit. And the opposite in a woman. If women find
> their integration easier than men, it may be because our
> culture is so male-oriented. No one will question a male
> emphasis. But if a man tries to emphasize the feminine, he
> may run into trouble. I mean an opposition from the man
> himself, an opposition that is typical of our kind of world.
> But it is no mere matter of a man being a little feminine now
> and then, allowing something soft and tender to emerge,

some show of tolerance and patience: qualities we think women favor. Or for a woman to be tough once in a while, as men are supposed to be tough. . . .

For we live in a man's world, my brothers, a man's world. I hope you have that clear. For if you have that clear, then you realize that woman is no great part of it. Not really. Even our prayer at the altar, even at the Eucharist, the love feast, we make it clear by the way we speak that it is a man's world. Which, of course, is not the world of Jesus or the Church. It is an aberration born of a breed of vultures who fed on decadence.

So if you would be Christian, you cannot go along with things as they are.[1]

This meditation was prompted by a fellow monk asking Father Matthew to serve as an impromptu dream interpreter of sorts; Matthew's conclusion was that "it looks as if [his] anima needs a little love, a little attention." This prompted his brother monk to admit that he was "not exactly in love with [his] feminine aspect," and then the quotation above.

It is not immediately clear what Father Matthew has in mind in venturing his criticism of this all-too-human Church. Criticisms of religious patriarchy are easily made, and usually well founded, but it would seem odd for a monk committed to withdrawal from the world, and thus most contact with women, to make them. The monastery is a man's world, after all. "Flute Solo" is a work of solitude. And monks, moreover, all of them men, must be celibate. Perhaps that is the place to start, then, with celibacy:

> The question of celibacy is discussed often on too shallow a level, and surely so if the mystical level is dismissed. To do that is to reduce celibacy to an act of prowess which as likely as not can end only in ruining the person. Celibacy without a deep love affair is a disaster. It is not even celibacy. It's just

---

[1] Matthew Kelty, "Dreaming," in *My Song is of Mercy*, 161–62.

not getting married. And the world has enough such people, married and otherwise.[2]

Just three pages later,[3] Father Matthew notices an intriguing connection between dawn and dusk: they are experienced as especially fitting times for prayer and for lovemaking (later, he will also equate celebrating the liturgy with making love).[4] This curious connection, between prayerful awakening and erotic ecstasy, leads him to the striking conclusion: "To monks religion is not patriarchal. It is fraternal, communal, brotherhood."[5] So he seems to have resolved his own cautionary word about this being a man's world; the monastery aspires to be a man's world with more lateral than vertical relations, a community of loving-kindness.

But how? We would do well to recall that the Gospel—precisely because it does not accept the metaphor of law for human relations, neither for politics nor for ethics—does not utilize checklists as a means for assessing moral virtue. A celibate is not someone who does not have sexual relations. Consider the reaction of a wife whose husband proudly declares at supper, "Honey, I was faithful to you today." Fidelity is a virtue, a lifelong aspiration and orientation; it is not something defined by what one does or does not do day-by-day. It is in this sense that celibacy is not "an act of prowess." It is rather an expression of a deeper kind of love affair, the passionate commitment to and desire for the divine. "Marriage is the usual meeting place of man and woman, of the head and the heart," Father Matthew observes:

> But the monk encounters woman in the bride of Christ, the church, his spouse. Yet the contact with her must be one in

[2] Matthew Kelty, "Flute Solo," in *My Song is of Mercy*, 47.
[3] Kelty, "Flute Solo," 50.
[4] Matthew Kelty, "Making Love in Liturgy," in *Sermons in a Monastery*, 70–74.
[5] Matthew Kelty, "Beyond Gender," in *Gethsemani Homilies*, 3.

which the individual is not overwhelmed by her. There must indeed be genuine contact, a real meeting, but only that. For the fire of love will burn bright only when the meeting is right. Only then is the poet set free, the contemplative, the mystic.[6]

It is startling to see how he makes his connections. The monk is married by sacred vow to the Church, a church Matthew imagines as feminine. Through this mystic marriage the monk touches fire, becomes poet and mystic, realizes his anima in the spirit of this heated union.

One of the more striking aspects of Father Matthew's social teachings, as it were, is how obediently he accepted most Catholic teachings regarding sex, celibacy, the marital union, contraception, and abortion. He did so in uncharacteristically strident tones:

> Mockery is a great weapon. There are about two-and-a-half million weddings a year in our land. *Bride's Magazine* says their readers spend about $13,000 on a wedding. 190 guests is the average number. Yet half these weddings will end in divorce. No wonder some young people do not bother with a wedding.
>
> And since most married people use birth control, mockery is made of love: there are flowers but no fruit. And since control is such a hoax, 50% of the million-and-a-half abortions in a year stem from contraceptive failure. So one mockery leads to another. It is called Planned Parenthood.[7]

Some of this is a question of personal[8] conviction and personal point of view. The Roman Catholic Church in the 1960s was

---

[6] Matthew Kelty, "Searching for the Heart," in *Sermons in a Monastery*, 67.

[7] Matthew Kelty, "Mockery," in *My Song is of Mercy*, 190.

[8] Father Matthew's especially poignant personal reasons for opposing abortion—namely, that his mother seriously considered aborting him—may be found in "Abortion: A Personal Experience," in *Gethsemani Homilies*, 120–21.

as riven as the rest of the country by dramatic shifts in social norms concerning gender, sexuality, and the conduct of the war. The question here is how an altogether iconoclastic monk, one part poet and one part mystic, came to possess such a traditional sexual ethic.

The question is compounded by the fact that Father Matthew was both non-conforming and gay. He described himself often as a rather quiet and effeminate youth, disinclined to sports and aggressive pursuits, more inclined to solitude and drawn to gentleness, especially gentleness in other men. The monastic environment attracted him instantly. For here he found a community of men in touch with their "feminine aspect," or at least trying to be so. "Nor," he adds in a moment of transparent self-reflection, "do I hesitate to say that this has some relationship to homosexuality."[9] As he grappled further with these conundrums and connections, he came to see a further connection: "It would appear to me, then, that if one sees birth control licit, one must also concede liberty to homosexual love."[10] Yet Father Matthew seemed to support neither, though his opposition was managed with compassion and deep concern, and his heart positively ached for the victims of homophobic outrage then rife in the land.[11] "Probably the closest anyone in our society comes to the Samaritan is the gay," he notes. "Not many, monks included, cotton to gays."[12]

When cultural reaction against gay men in the United States had reached a fever pitch (Eve Kosofsky Sedgwick ominously referred to 1986 as "open season on gay men"[13]), Father Matthew penned one of his most luminous short essays: "Celibacy and

[9] Kelty, "Flute Solo," 54 (go to 58).

[10] Kelty, "Flute Solo," 69.

[11] Matthew Kelty, "For Eric," in *My Song is of Mercy*, 136–38.

[12] Matthew Kelty, "Hiroshima Day," in *The Call of Wild Geese*, 73.

[13] Eve Kosofsky Sedgwick, *Epistemology of the Closet* (Berkeley, CA: University of California Press, 1990), 31.

the Gift of Gay."[14] He begins, as we might expect by now, with anima, now more closely defined:

> Jung spoke of the other side of man as his anima, the collective center of all we think of as feminine when we think as males. And this feminine is not merely pragmatic or diversional, but is also numinous, just as male-female love has overtones of immortality. It is this intense experience of the other side of man, the feminine side, that is basic—in my view—to an understanding of what it is to be gay. (256)

And so he returns to the question of celibacy—viewed now as a state of mind, not an act of prowess:

> The man (and the woman, in the other court), who experiences some sense of call to celibacy is playing with a number of factors which may be much mixed in the beginning: he is lonely, he is different, he has a strong religious sense, he wants others, he wants a point and purpose and a reason to live. And he needs love. Merely assuming that a gay man seeks an integration of all that he is, does beg a question: Why bother? If most men are consumed with questions of meaning and significance, and who says this is so, the gay man is most likely to be so, in depth, by reason of a bi-polarity experienced in measure. Opposing forces generate heat and light. . . .
>
> Who by virtue of the gift of faith knows the love of God, the service of God, do not surprise us by gravitating to the celibate state, the consecrated life, since it unites the search for integrity and wholeness with a superb direction and purpose, the love of brothers, the spiritual context, God? Who better qualified for celibacy than the gay? (257)

This is a quite remarkable turnabout: gay men are the profoundest and most suitable candidates for the call to sacred

---

[14] This is the Epilogue to *My Song is of Mercy*, 256–59. All subsequent quotations cited in parentheses come from this essay.

celibacy. Their very advancement on the path of integration equips them for the lifelong perspective:

> I may as well make it clear: heterosexuals find all this very difficult . . . a heterosexual style of male love will be assumed normal [for celibates]. Which is fun when you are 20 with an unsure ego, dull by the time you are 30, and deathly in your 40s. Which is why so many heterosexuals abandon celibacy after a decade or two: they cannot handle it; they need an external woman to awaken the inner one, especially in our culture. Perhaps in a less divided one they would do better. (258)

And yet we should wonder, and worry: is the idea that, since their sexual expression is disallowed by the Church, then gays are most suited to celibacy? Is it the only way to inhabit their anima and still remain Christian?

This is decidedly not Father Matthew's view. For this kind of ethical reasoning about sexuality and celibacy not only relies upon the checklist-reasoning I mentioned earlier; still worse, it fails to distinguish between love and sex (and sensuality):[15]

> And since those who tend to worry will worry here about sex, the answer is simple: sex is no problem. Love is. Where there is no love you can expect sex to emerge. All men want love, celibates too. Sex can be one way of loving, but it is absurd to say: no sex is no love, as absurd as saying sex is love. (259)

One cannot escape the feeling that Father Matthew is recalling Thomas Merton here, Merton, whose passionate love affair with a nearby nurse in his fifty-second year caused a great deal of turmoil to man and monastery alike.[16] Some years before

---

[15] Kelty, "Making Love in Liturgy," 70–74.

[16] See Merton's remarkably frank and endearingly passionate reflections in the sixth volume of his published journals, *Learning to Love*, ed. Christine

that affair, Merton came to one of his periodic spiritual insights, and recalled it in a journal entry that is among his most quoted, and most memorable (it was March 1958):

> Yesterday, in Louisville, at the corner of 4th and Walnut, I suddenly realized that I loved all the people and that none of them were or could be totally alien to me. As if waking from a dream—the dream of my separateness, of the "special" vocation to be different. . . . I am still a member of the human race—and what a glorious destiny is there for man, since the Word was made flesh and became, too, a member of the Human Race!
>
> Thank God! Thank God! I am only another member of the human race. . . . I have the immense joy of being a man! As if the sorrows of our condition could really matter, once we begin to realize who and what we are—as if we could ever begin to realize it on earth.
>
> It is not a question of proving to myself that I either dislike or like the women one sees in the street. The fact of having a vow of chastity does not oblige one to argument on this point—no special question arises. I am keenly conscious, not of their beauty (I hardly think I saw anyone really beautiful by special standards) but of their humanity, their womanness. But what incomprehensible beauty is there, what secret beauty that would perhaps be inaccessible to me if I were not dedicated to a different way of life. It is as though by chastity I had come to be unafraid of what is most pure in all the women of the world and to taste and sense the secret beauty of their girls' hearts as they walked in the sunlight— each one secret and good and lovely in the sight of God— never touched by anyone, nor by me, nor by anyone, as good

---

M. Bochen (New York: HarperSanFrancisco, 1997). The affair lasted from April to September of 1966, when it was discovered by the abbot. Of special note is the separate June books that Merton composed for her, entitled "A Midsummer Diary for M" (301–48). See also Mark Shaw, *Beneath the Mask of Loneliness: Thomas Merton and the Forbidden Love Affair that Set Him Free* (New York: Palgrave Macmillan, 2009).

as and even more beautiful than life itself. For the woman-ness that is in each of them is at once original and inexhaust-ibly fruitful, bringing the image of God into the world. In this each one is Wisdom and Sophia and Our Lady.[17]

The relentlessly heterosexual dimension of this revelation is deafening after listening to Father Matthew's view of things. This important essay on celibacy and the gay gift is clearly engaged in a difficult dialogue, not just with the mainstream culture, but with Merton the man. There is even evidence to suggest that Father Matthew considered Thomas Merton homo-phobic, and resolutely so.[18] Still, we must dig a bit deeper.

I began with Father Matthew's cautionary word to his fellow monks that theirs was a man's world and the feminine was too often excluded from it—at great spiritual cost: "Even our prayer at the altar, even at the Eucharist, the love feast, we make it clear by the way we speak that it is a man's world." Even at prayer? Does he mean the references to Father and Son? If so, then the Roman Church, unlike its Protestant counterparts,[19] has a significant spiritual resource: namely, the cult of Mary, Our Lady, to whom all Cistercian monasteries are dedicated.

I have already discussed Father Matthew's rich and remark-able reflections on time when considering the Immaculate Conception of Mary. The richness of his lifelong reflections on Mary was remarkable. Referring to the Romantic and Disney-land need for happy endings, Father Matthew allows us some space for fairy tales: they are "meant to be a bridge to the land

[17] Thomas Merton, *The Intimate Merton: His Life from His Journals*, ed. Patrick Hart and Jonathan Montaldo (New York: HarperCollins Publishers, 1996), 124–25.

[18] See the anonymous reference by Peter Savastano, "Thomas Merton Saved My Life and Opened My Heart to What It Really Means to Be Truly 'Catholic'," in *We Are Already One: Thomas Merton's Message of Hope*, ed. Gray Henry and Jonathan Montaldo (Louisville, KY: Fons Vitae, 2015), 178. It is instructive that Savastano does not agree with this assessment.

[19] Matthew Kelty, "The Virgin," in *My Song is of Mercy*, 59.

of faith." In Mary's story, Matthew adduces elements of a fairy tale:

> Jesus is ours by way of a woman. The woman's name is Mary. By virtue of what she was called to be, she was conceived without sin. That is Part I. Part II is that she conceived of the Holy Spirit and became by that fact the mother of Jesus Christ, son of God. Part III is that Christ was born of her nine months later in the nativity of God on earth. Part IV is the climax of her Assumption into heaven which it is our joy to celebrate today. They are all of a piece, all parts of a whole that necessarily go together. They are all essential.
>
> They have a fairy-tale quality. That is, they are in some ways incredible; in other ways, essential to the faith story.[20]

The fairy tale only lasts so long as you forget the heart of the story; let us call it Part IIIb: the crucifixion of her son. Mary lived to see what all parents dread: the death of her child in a manner as gruesome as it was public. "Yet she was there when we crucified her Lord. And heard him forgive us. And heard him commend us to her care."[21]

Mary's story is not fairy tale; it is tragedy. And compassion is the capacity that tragedy enables: "In our suffering too, we shall grow closer to the Mother of God. Nothing softens the

[20] Matthew Kelty, "Mary," in *Gethsemani Homilies*, 92.

[21] Matthew Kelty, "The Virgin," in *My Song is of Mercy,* 62. Strikingly and stridently, he relates this to his anti-abortion views: "The age of abortion, divorce, sterilization, can scarcely be an age of reverence for women. Rather it is barbarous in this as it is in its love for violence, massive wars, greed, oppression, contempt for human life and human rights. In such a nightmare, a call for devotion to Our Lady seems almost pointless." And again: "Thus, a so-called patriarchal Church is also very feminine. Since faith is expressed in prayer and revealed in action, it is no wonder that nobody on earth has done more for women and carries on today, often alone, in a world that trivializes sex, perverts marriage, and puts life to death in a new barbarism" (Matthew Kelty, "The New Eve," in *Singing for the Kingdom*, 111).

heart as does pain."[22] So Mary is the feminine side to the masculine divine, the infinite compassion that enables tragic forgiveness and reconciling love. She is the anima.

And Matthew loved her adoringly.

---

[22] Kelty, *My Song is of Mercy*, 61.

7. Ecstasy

Ring the bells that still can ring.
Forget your perfect offering.
There is a crack in everything.
That's how the light gets in.

Leonard Cohen, "Anthem" (1992)

The soul can split the sky in two,
And let the face of God shine through.

Edna St. Vincent Millay, "Renascence" (1917)

❖ ❖ ❖ ❖ ❖

Father Matthew appears to have come across this poem by Edna St. Vincent Millay in the spring of 1991; he quotes it several times in the succeeding months.[1] It is a soaring account of human possibility, the raw power of anima. And it is Romantic to the core.

I would like to recall Charles Sprawson's remarkable cultural history of swimming here, with its notable historical benchmarks: the Greeks and Romans swam, the Christians turned away from the sea, and the Romantics returned to her soft embrace.

There is an intriguing sexual subtext to Sprawson's cultural history, and it hinges on male homoerotic desire. To put it

---

[1] Matthew Kelty, *My Song is of Mercy*, 208, 213.

rather crudely, Sprawson seems to believe that Greek and Roman swimmers were gay (or rather, bisexual) and that the Christians turned away from this romantic idyll just as surely as they turned away from the water. The Romantics, many of the most preeminent swimmers and writers among them, were also gay or bisexual, thereby alienated from the dominant cultural norms and reacting to this sense of obliqueness with a far more private orientation, pursuing lives in solitude. There is significant overlap between Sprawson's analysis of the "psychology of the swimmer"[2] and Father Matthew's analysis of the gay male anima. There is deep spiritual solitude here, in the water and in the monastery.

But there is a significant caveat to be made, just here. Father Matthew was talking about love, not sex; he was also talking about anima, not the warm frolic of bodily eroticism. We should parse these differences carefully.

Plato famously argued, in an altogether audacious philosophical discussion of love,[3] that madness is a gift from the gods. Like Father Matthew, he too felt it important to make some distinctions. He lists a number of experiences that we can only call spiritual, or religious, in this context: oracular pronouncement, prophetic insight, poetic inspiration . . . monastic work, as Father Matthew would have us see it (or else flute music). But, to echo the apostle Paul, Plato concludes that the greatest of these gifts is love. The word he uses is *eros*; the question of how to translate this word into English is an enormously challenging, and enormously fruitful, question to pursue. "Passionate desire" may get us closer to the semantic field, I think.

But the word does not appear in the New Testament, and, like most such ellipses, this silence is very difficult to translate. Some think that the Christians were simply allergic to Greek *eros* and tried to avoid it altogether; this is Sprawson's view of

---

[2] Charles Sprawson, *Haunts of the Black Masseur*, 17ff.
[3] Plato, *Phaedrus* 244a–245c.

the matter. Others think that it simply was not a matter of deep cultural interest or concern for the early church; John Boswell made important contributions to this view of the matter.[4] Others think that the Christian subculture simply adopted another, more peripheral and more obscure Greek word, *agape*, and adopted it as its own; this is the word, and perhaps the worldview, Paul favors. The differentiation between *eros* and *agape* has, in any case, enabled some significant and creative theological reflection.[5]

I would like to suggest that Father Matthew seemed drawn to the idea of *eros* as ecstasy, spiritual ecstasy, the dance of poetic anima. I am thinking of Bernini's audacious sculpture, "The Ecstasy of St. Theresa," with its frankly erotic, and even orgasmic, depiction of spiritual transport. There is a great deal of medieval mystical reflection that can be marshaled to defend the orthodoxy of this depiction.[6] Father Matthew's writings may be read in a similar spiritual vein. Claiming to be neither scholar nor translator, Father Matthew in his lyrical body of written work shows himself to be both. His inspired meditations on how the organic elements combine in creatures capable of joyous ecstasy constitute the very foundation for all of his life and work. Even a casual survey of his writings confronts one with the astonishing fleshiness, sensuality, and I

---

[4] John Boswell, *Christianity, Social Tolerance and Homosexuality: A History of Gay People from Rome to the Fourteenth Century* (Chicago: The University of Chicago Press, 1980), 61–87. A nice summary of Boswell's work and its enduring importance may be found in *The Boswell Thesis: Essays on Christianity, Social Tolerance and Homosexuality*, ed. Matthew Kuefler (Chicago: The University of Chicago Press, 2006).

[5] The Swedish Protestant Anders Nygren initiated this discussion in 1930–1936 with his two-volume work, *Agape and Eros*, trans. Philip S. Watson (New York: Harper & Row, 1953). C. S. Lewis's *The Four Loves* (London: Geoffrey Bles, 1960) is perhaps better known.

[6] See, for instance, Caroline Walker Bynum, *Holy Feast and Holy Fast* (Berkeley, CA: University of California Press, 1986), 150–86, 245–59. It is noteworthy that the feminine anima was especially creative in its development of this trope.

daresay the eroticism, of his prose: lovemaking through liturgy, bread, wine, laughter, the communion of saints, the communion of monastic life, his passionate attachment to Mary.

But there is also the bass note of death that haunts his writing and clearly haunted him as a younger man. He was also (and equally) haunted by the present persistence of evil and of sin. His life's work was the work of transforming the fear of God into erotic desire for the divine. To live authentically and spiritually is to love in this fiery manner.

This too is an erotic insight. The point I am after here is perhaps best made by Anne Carson, the poet-philosopher whom I mentioned at the beginning of this book:

> Eros is an issue of boundaries. He exists because certain boundaries do. In the interval between reach and grasp, between glance and counterglance, between "I love you" and "I love you too," the absent presence of desire comes alive. But the boundaries of time and glance and I love you are only aftershocks of the main, inevitable boundary that creates Eros: the boundary of flesh and self between you and me. And it is only, suddenly, at the moment when I would dissolve that boundary, I realize I never can. . . .
>
> If we follow the trajectory of eros we consistently find it tracing this same route: it moves out from the lover toward the beloved, then ricochets back to the lover himself and the hole in him, unnoticed before. Who is the real subject of most love poems? Not the beloved. It is that hole.[7]

Eros is the divining rod that points to our incompleteness, the hole in us that takes time, and solitude, and passionate desire, to see clearly, then to appreciate, and ultimately to cultivate. We are cracked creatures, and as such, *pace* Leonard

---

[7] Anne Carson, *Eros the Bittersweet* (McLean, IL: Dalkey Archive Press, 1998), 30. I am currently completing a book-length manuscript devoted to Carson's erotic philosophy, entitled *Reach without Grasping: Anne Carson's Classical Desires* (London: Bloomsbury Academic, forthcoming).

Cohen, it is through our cracks that the divine light comes through. Our brokenness may be necessary to God, necessary to reconciliation; there must be a hole to fill; there must be some boundary to enable our transcendence. However intimately related our soul may be to divine spirit, there remains a gap, a hole, and this hole is holy, generating the desire to cross over. For Father Matthew, the love of God is erotically ecstatic or it is not at all.

In the end, for Father Matthew, there remained only this sure credo:

> We are surrounded by eternity. It is just over the ridge, just beneath my mind, within earshot. We live in it as surely, more surely than we live in time. We are eternal, time is not.[8]

Transparent, that is, to the everlasting mercy.

[8] Matthew Kelty, "Veterans Day," in *My Song is of Mercy*, 218.

Acknowledgments

This book has had many friends and sources of inspiration I would like to mention briefly here. First and foremost, Mike Bever and Brother Paul Quenon were central to my conception of the work and my ability to bring it off. As I said at the outset, I met Father Matthew through Mike and first saw his importance through Mike's filmic eyes. Brother Paul was the consummate host at Gethsemani; I recall our day together at Merton's hermitage with fondness and abiding gratitude.

I am grateful to all of the monks and staff at Gethsemani; to the degree that this book is an ethnography of modern monastic life, they are the insiders who let an outsider in and made him feel at home. I hope what is written here is true to the spirit of that place.

My new home Department of Anthropology at Georgia State University has brought new life and rejuvenation into my scholarly work. My debt to them runs deeper than lists allow, but it deserves naming. Sincere thanks, then, to Parris Baker, Steve Black, Jeffrey Glover, Ema Guano, Kathryn Kozaitis (our Chair), Faidra Papavasiliou, Jen Patico, Nicola Sharratt, Bethany Turner-Livermore, Chrislyn Turner, Cassandra White, Frank Williams, and Brent Woodfill.

I have served as Director of the Center for Hellenic Studies at my university for the past six years; it is a demanding job, but one that has brought a number of wonderful people into my life whom I'd not have known otherwise. I am moved to mention Margot Alexander, the Honorable Manos Androulakis, Jennie Burnet, Ryan Carlin, Nickitas Demos, Allen Fromherz,

Christos Galileias, the Honorable Vassilis Gouloussis, Father Paul Kaplanis of the Greek Cathedral of the Annunciation, Annie Latta, Bill Long, Leslie Marsh, Pearl McHaney, Ghulam Nadri, George Nakos, Tony Lemieux, the Honorable Giorgos Panayiotidis, Father Panayiotis Papagiorgiou of the Holy Transfiguration Greek Orthodox Church, Dean Sara Rosen, Lindsay Samson, Maria Sharp, Shamieca Shine, Despina Soteres, and Golfo Vastakis.

Former students and other close friends who enrich my daily life here in Atlanta include Wesley Barker, Mary Grace Dupree, Jill Eady, Aikaterina Grigoriadou, Andrew Lee, Barbara Marston, Laura McKee, Natasha Patel, Alessandra Raengo, John Rivenbark, Sarah Levine, Larry Slutsker, Cassandra Velasco, and Bill and Carol Winkler. A life in the university may lack the choreographed disciplinary calendar of a monastery, but the regularity with which I am able to see them gives more than order to my days; it brings me joy.

There are three friends in Atlanta whom I see less regularly, but our meetings are all the more precious for that fact. Paul Courtright, Jack Fitzmier, and Gary Laderman have been my professional and personal lodestars for the past decade. Jack is retiring as this book goes to press and will be moving to Madison, Wisconsin, soon thereafter. Our circle will be incomplete without him, but he, much like the monk who discerns the virtues of solitude, is moving closer to his center. We share his joy in that fact.

The staff of the Vatican Library and Secret Archives have welcomed me with extraordinary warmth into their community for the past twelve years. Much of what I know about the Catholic Church—its deep intellectual traditions, its cosmopolitan ethos and capacity for care—I learned in its Library . . . which tells you something. I am especially indebted to Drs. Christina Grafinger, Luigina Orlandi, and Paolo Vian for their countless graces to me over many years.

And finally, a book is not a book without a production team. I extend my warmest thanks to the good people at Cistercian

Publications, especially my editor, Marsha Dutton, and the superb production staff, including Hans Christoffersen, Stephanie Lancour, and Colleen Stiller.

LAR
Atlanta, GA

Appendix

This is a letter that Father Matthew addressed to me, after our first visit, which Michael Bever arranged. I had sent him my first book in thanks for our visit.

Wednesday
September 19, '07

Dear Dr. Ruprecht,

Thank you for "Tragic Posture and Tragic Vision." I write you at once, for I have 2 nieces coming tomorrow from California for a visit. If I put off a response, I may forget it altogether. I read the chapter on the Parthenon. Because it is interesting. And there is a copy of it in Nashville, TN. For a "worlds fair" years ago. I believe the Virgin Mary took over for a time. The version in Nashville has the original goddess—or a copy I should say.

You live in another word—of scholars + scholarship. The abbey here has a few scholars, but they are exceptional. But I don't think there is any conflict between being a monk and a scholar. Or being married + scholarly.

What amazes me is that Europe, for all its chaotic history of war + division + domination, still remains a land of rich memories, treasuries of the past.

A German brother once vexed me for saying that "Americans are Kulturlos"—no culture. What he meant of course, was that we have no history. We are so newly come on the map. All of Europe is ancient.

I send you love + thanks.

God bless your scholarship. Carry on for the glory of God. And the common good.

Come by again some time
Fr. Matthew

Note: There are many reasons to treasure a letter such as this. The care with which it was crafted, a care belied by its casual brevity, is startling. Father Matthew began, not only by addressing my book, but by zeroing in on one of its central interests: namely, the continuity between the "pagan" and Christian periods in Greece. He then undercut the depth of his insight and engagement, by claiming not to be a scholar, himself. Then he countered, admitting that a monk could be a scholar (like Merton, like him). And that a scholar could be married (as he clearly wished me to be). Next he turned my interest in Greece to his interest in the Celts: "All of Europe is ancient." He then concluded with a gentle evangelical reminder: to consider my work in the service of God . . . and the common good. Here is poetry, poignancy, and passion, combined. Here is spirit as well. "No scholar," indeed.